IT'S JUST A NOSEBLEED

My Long Journey

FRANCES MOULT, STAFF NURSE

authorHOUSE®

AuthorHouse™ UK Ltd.
1663 Liberty Drive
Bloomington, IN 47403 USA
www.authorhouse.co.uk
Phone: 0800.197.4150

Published by AuthorHouse 08/14/2013

ISBN: 978-1-4918-0414-8 (sc)
ISBN: 978-1-4918-0415-5 (e)

This book is printed on acid-free paper.

CHAPTER 1

It's 4 a.m. on a January morning. It's very dark outside and very cold. I'm in a bed on a hospital ward writing in the dark and thinking about my journey over the last three years through the ups and downs of life as a staff nurse, mother, grandmother, and patient. Although I can't really see what I'm writing, but I feel it inside.

It started in January 2009; a lot happened, what a bad start to the year. One of my dear friends was found dead in her chair on a Monday morning. She had suffered from lung cancer, but only for a few months—so quickly, so little time. On the Saturday before she died, she rang me and asked me to bring the kids over" she said. Meaning my youngest son and my two grandchildren. She had looked after them when they were small. Yes even my son who was 20 years old by this time. We were also at the same school, although she was in the year ahead of me, so we go a long way back.

I accepted the invitation, and on the next day, we all went to visit her. I was quite shocked to see her sitting with oxygen beside her.; she had not needed oxygen before; this development happened quickly. We chatted and laughed as we watched my granddaughters play; she had bought them each a present. She then decided to have a cigarette, and her son literally flew across the room.

"Mum, you can't have one!"

"Yes I can," she replied, giving me a mischievous grin. As she pulled out a cigarette, her son rushed to remove her mask and turned off the oxygen before she blew us all up.

A little later, we finished our drinks, and it was time for my family to leave, as my friend looked very tired. As I hugged her goodbye, she whispered to me. "I have always and will always love you."

"I love you too," I said. I didn't think too much of those words, as we had said them before.

The next morning, I went to work as usual, and at 9 a.m., I received a call from my friend's son: my friend was gone. I sat in the staff room and just cried. The nursing staff were all there with me, understanding how I felt about the loss of such a dear person. I left my car at work as one of my colleagues then took me home, as I was not in a good place or in the right frame of mind to drive. My hubby went and picked up my car later with my son in law.

My friend's death was very tragic. She was so shocked at her cancer diagnosis that she had lost her footing on the stairs in the hospital and ended up breaking her hip, so she could do nothing about the cancer until they fixed her hip.

I attended her funeral saying goodbye to my lovely friend along with a lot of people; as she was very well loved and would be sorely missed. I kissed a red rose and laid it on her coffin as she was lowered into the ground. My heart ached for her and her caring, loving husband and son.

On Mother's Day the same year, my poor dog Cleo had collapsed. She was seventeen. I had come downstairs in the morning half asleep and there she was lying by the front door like a fur rug, with all her limbs stretched out. I called to my husband, and he came running down the stairs, she was still alive, and my husband and I sat with her and hugged her for a while, and then we took her to the vet's.

The vet determined that my dog had had a stroke but that we should give her a chance to recover as she had never been ill in her life. My husband and I were in full agreement with that. The vet gave her an injection, and we took her home. It was so sad to watch her—she swung her head side to side, she became incontinent, and just looked so ragged. We had to coax her to eat. She had been with my family since my son was about four years old, so even though he was now a young man he cried as he watched her.

One morning after my dog came home; she sat beside me and just looked at me as if to say, "Please, I've had enough." Her eyes looked so sad. My family determined we should put Cleo to sleep. We took her for a walk before getting her in the car, and she seemed to perk up, which made me wonder if we were doing the right thing going back to the vets. But ten minutes later, she drooped again,. It was a Sunday, and we had difficulty finding a vet whose office was open, but we finally found one with very kind staff members. When we arrived, the staff took us into the clinic. My husband and I stayed with her as she was put to sleep. It was heartbreaking, and I cried. "I'm so sorry darling," I said, remembering her as a pup, the runt of the litter, tiny enough to carry in my pocket. Before she came to live with us, I didn't want a dog in the house again, but then, on a visit to a friend her dog had had pups, this runt climbed up on my lap, and that was it. I took her home. What a loyal pet she was, full of mischief and love.

Then, in April that year, my daughter, who was only twenty-four, became ill due to a growth in the right side of the main artery of the brain. All that went through my mind in the months following was that I was going to lose her. I went to see her each day after work, spending all my time either working or with her.

When a consultant came to see her, I asked him questions, and he answered a few, and then he said that he needed to operate to find out exactly what was in my daughter's brain, as scans showed a mass around the artery that the consultant believed was non-cancerous but could still be dangerous. We sat in the hospital's day room for several hours while surgeons performed a craniotomy. No one came to see if we wanted tea or to tell us my daughter was in recovery—the staff said nothing, leaving me to worry, and I felt an unbelievable resentment for the staff's lack of care. I understood that the doctors and nurses caring for my daughter looked after a very busy ward, and worked long hours, but as a nurse, I expected them to provide more help for worried relatives, as is my usual practice. Perhaps I was being unfair to think like that. But that's the way I felt at that time, who knows?

My worry over my child's condition superseded all other thoughts, and my mind was in turmoil. Finally, after so many hours, of sitting I sought out a nurse, and she told me my daughter was on her way back to the ward. A bit later, I went to see my daughter, and she was wide awake.

"I want a cigarette," she said. We laughed, and I was relieved that she seemed fine.

"You'll have to wait, baby," I told her. "You have only just got back from the operating theatre."

She glared at me, got out of bed, and put on her dressing grown. "Are you coming?" she said.

We had to laugh again. This was my feisty girl. We all went with her outside for a cigarette.

In the days after my daughter's operation, she phoned me several times, crying in pain. One morning she rang and told me she was sitting on the kerb by the outpatients' department. She was in a lot of pain, and I told her to get pain relief, but she said the nurses had told her to wait for it because they were too busy. I was very upset and angry by then, so I phoned the ward to ask how she was. The nurse said my daughter was fine. So I asked.

"If that's correct," I said, "why is she sitting outside the front entrance crying in pain?"

The nurse had no answer for me because, as she then explained that, the staff didn't realise my daughter was not on the ward. I then rang my sister-in-law, and she dropped everything and flew to the hospital. She helped get my daughter treatment for her pain. What a treasure my sister-in-law is.

My daughter was diagnosed with Tolosa-Hunt syndrome, a neurological illness. I've read that the exact cause is not known but that the disorder is thought to be associated with inflammation of the areas behind the eyes. To treat my daughter's condition, her doctor prescribed a few bouts of chemotherapy, although sometimes she was unable to undergo the treatment because her blood tests were too abnormal. The chemo made my daughter so sick. She went quite blind in one eye and on occasion wore an eye patch for protection. She was also prescribed steroids which made her weight balloon, making her very angry. I don't blame her for her anger and frustration with what she was going through. My heart was heavy, as I didn't know how to give her any comfort, as she would push me and other carers away.

When my daughter came home from hospital, I would hear her screaming in the night with the pain in her head. *God help her,* I thought. *I'm a staff nurse, and I'm useless; I can't even help my baby.* She told me then that it was usual for the pain to be violent for a time but that it would settle down with pain relief—and she requested that I leave her alone to deal with it herself. By this time she was taking morphine. Also at this time I was still at work. My dear colleagues supported me as I spent a lot of time in the office in tears.

Through all that year's events, I carried on with work and my daily routines, just with these added extras thrown in. I had no rest running after everything and everybody, but I didn't want to rest. I didn't want to have the time to think. I wondered how my mum had felt when my nineteen-year-old brother died in a bike accident and whether she had felt the way I felt? I was too scared to think about it. I wouldn't have been able to cope if I lost one of my babies. My mind was always busy with worry. At times I would arrive at work without knowing how I got there. Why were all these things happening? One thing after another, when would they stop?

My boss always kept an eye on me waiting and ready to offer help if I needed it. She suggested that I might want to talk to someone about what I was going through and how I was feeling. Eventually I agreed after thinking about it and went to see a therapist. She was a nice lady who wasn't intrusive, but, then, she also didn't talk much. Having never seen a therapist before, I wasn't too sure what to expect. I went to three sessions over the next few weeks but didn't feel any different, so I decided that seeing a therapist was not for me and that I could probably cope quite well on my own.

When my daughter recovered, she decided she wanted to become a carer herself because of what she had gone through. She got a job, to my surprise, on the very ward she had been a patient in. She loved working there, and appeared very happy although she still suffered from intermittent violent headaches. I was pleased with her choice and proud of her.

While my daughter was ill, I began to miss having a dog around the house. Our family always had a pet of some kind whist the children were young, even though my husband and I did most of the cleaning up after them. In addition to our dog, one of the girls had two gerbils; one had two guinea pigs, Pebbles and Bamm-Bamm, and she was devoted to them; and one had a rabbit. My husband and I agreed to get another dog, so we went to the Dogs Trust to search for a dog that needed a good home. The staff were very kind and also insistent that the dogs in their care went to good homes, so we wandered around the kennels and studied the dogs' behaviour until we found one that we felt would be perfect with us. We had to wait for him until the Trust was satisfied that we would be good owners, and then home he came. His name is Blaize and we were delighted to find him to be the perfect addition to our family; he likes to run fast around the fields by our house in a short quick burst, and then for the rest of the day he lazes around the house. He also has very soft fur and likes a lot of loving.

CHAPTER 2

In May, I started getting the odd bout of dizziness accompanied by nosebleeds. When the first one struck, I had been playing with my dog and thought he had scratched my nose, hence the nose bleeds. But the bouts continued after that. One day at work, my nose was hurting a little and the dizziness was more intense than usual, so I went to see my boss. And how stupid did I think I sounded? "I have a sore nose and need to go off sick" sounded so lame to me, but I didn't feel right working, so I had no choice but to leave. I went to my doctor after that and several more times, explaining I had nose bleeds and all I could smell was blood. He gave me several courses of antibiotics but nothing helped.

All through the next few months, the nosebleeds continued. The bleeding wasn't heavy or continuous, but it was consistent each day. I suspected I had a problem, as my training as a nurse I know that this was not normal, and as a person I know my own body. I had never had nosebleeds before. I requested that my doctor refer me to an ear, nose, and throat specialist (ENT) at the hospital. My doctor seemed unconcerned.

"It's just a nosebleed," he said. "You just need the right antibiotics." Several times over the next few weeks I asked for a referral again, but my doctor seemed not to be listening to me and wouldn't give me a referral, perhaps he didn't believe me about my nosebleeds because I had seen him previously complaining of flu-like symptoms and suspecting that I had swine flu. He didn't even look in my nose.

The nosebleeds continued, and in March of 2010 the nose bleeds continued, so I changed surgeries and explained the problem to the new doctor. She was very kind and understanding. She prescribed another week of antibiotics and said that if they didn't help, she would refer me to the ENT. I agreed. In June, after the course of antibiotics had failed, the doctor sent me to hospital. The ENT consultant, a lovely man whom I had had the pleasure of working with in his clinic several years earlier, checked my nose and then asked me if I picked my nose. I laughed and said, "No way." The consultant then recommended surgery to diagnose the problem. Five days later, I went to the operating theatre. It was an easy procedure: the consultant took a biopsy, a common test in which a surgeon takes a sample of tissue to determine the presence or extent of a disease, and I felt no pain. I went straight back to work feeling well.

I went to the outpatient department to see the consultant for the results a week later. He told me that the results from the biopsy weren't clear and asked if he could get another. I agreed, and five days later, I went back to the theatre, and this time, as the consultant told me afterwards, he took several samples. I felt no pain and encountered no problems, and again I went back to work, but the nosebleeds continued. On a coffee break with the girls at work, we discussed my operations, and I explained that I was going to see the ENT consultant again in a few days. I laughed and said, "I bet he tells me its cancer."

Just a joke!. But when I went to the follow-up appointment, my hubby came with me. We sat down, and the consultant looked at me at said, "I'm so sorry. This is very hard for me, but we found malignant cells in the biopsies." He gave me a diagnosis of squamous cell carcinoma of the septum, an infrequent condition that is often misdiagnosed because its symptoms are similar to everyday complaints. We thanked the consultant, and I said, "Okay, what do I do now?"

The consultant explained that he would refer me to head and neck specialists, and then my hubby and I went home to wait. On the way home, I asked him what he was thinking. "Nothing," he said. He didn't really know what to say, and neither did I. We tried to discuss the diagnosis more after we got home, as he does not like discussions of this kind it did not last too long. I didn't feel shocked or too upset, although I felt angry at my previous GP for not listening to me, and in hindsight, I think I already knew that I would be diagnosed with cancer anyway. I told my husband that if I had to go through all this, then there was no one else I'd rather go through it with, and we hugged. I went to have a bath to relax and think quietly. As I soaked, I thought of my mum and missed her so much. I talk to her whilst I'm lying there,

"I think I've had it, Mum," I said. "Please be there waiting for me." I laughed at myself. "Don't be stupid." I cried silently. I didn't know what to feel and couldn't, didn't want to think right now. I had always been fit; I grew up causing the usual problems, getting into scrapes. I loved to swim and was on the diving team at school. There were days when Mum and Dad would take my siblings and me to a local pavilion park, which was miles long, being that it was also a golf course, for picnics and blackberry picking. I loved the green and would sit in a tree for hours reading, enjoying the peace away from what was going on at home. Beginning when I was eight and continuing until I was sixteen, I was a member of the St John Ambulance Brigade, as my dream was to become a nurse. This all seemed a lifetime ago.

The head and neck specialists' office were very quick in setting my first appointment at the hospital within two weeks. My hubby came with me, but I was still quite nervous. The specialist asked how I was and was very kind as he explained that I would need to undergo a couple of scans so that he could determine the extent of the cancer.

A week later, I had an MRI and a CT scan to check my whole body. According to the web page "MRI Scan" on *NHS Choices*, "Magnetic resonance imaging (MRI) is a type of scan used to diagnose health conditions that affect organs, tissue and bone. MRI scanners use strong magnetic fields to produce detailed images of the inside of the body. An MRI scanner is a large tube … You lie inside the tube during the scan. An MRI scan is used to investigate almost any part of the body", and the images it produces can show signs of a mass easily (http://www.nhs.uk/Conditions/MRI-scan/Pages/Introduction.aspx). A CT scan, sometimes referred to as a CAT scan, also produces images of structures inside the body, including the internal organs, blood vessels, bones, and tumours. Following my scans, the specialist found no cancer anywhere other than in my septum, so that was a relief.

I next went to the operating theatre yet again to have my septum removed. After the operation, I stayed in hospital only one night, and when I woke, two of my girls were sitting beside me. I smiled at them although I felt a lot of pain and had some bleeding. However, when the doctor came to see me on his round, he didn't seem too concerned, and he discharged me, sending me home with pain relief.

A week after my surgery, my husband and I went back to the hospital for my follow-up appointment. The specialist looked in my nose with a camera, which was a bit uncomfortable but not painful. He explained that he had removed my septum completely along with an extra margin for safety because I had an aggressive type of cancer and the regrowth rate was high. For this reason, I would also need to have radiotherapy within six weeks to prevent the cancer from growing again. He said he had also sent the tissues he had removed for testing, and we hoped the results came back with good news. I asked him if I would have had to go through this intensive treatment if the cancer had been found earlier, and he responded that that might have been the case but that this type of cancer could be hard to spot.

After my surgery doctors had suggested that I wear a prosthesis that glued onto my nose, which could be made to look natural with a little foundation. In pictures of people wearing them on the Internet, they look all right, but I wasn't sure I liked the idea of it. Then it came into my head I thought, *What if I sneeze in public? The prosthesis will blow off in the street!* I had made up my mind—no way was I going to wear one. The lady specialist that makes and fits them was very nice but was not too pleased when I said no. I laughed about it afterwards and explained my feelings about it to my family, and when they saw the issue from my point of view that I felt bad enough already and might feel worse if I embarrassed myself by losing the prosthesis in public, and they agreed with my decision.

Still, I had to have a different sort of prosthesis, a very small, round object, fitted in my nose to keep the nostrils open. Taking it out to clean it and then putting it back in was horrid. When I went back to work, as the hospital staff had requested, and the ward sisters were fascinated by it and tried to look up my nose while we chatted prior to my shift. I didn't mind; in fact, I found it rather amusing. The ward sisters were worried about whether I would cope, but I assured them I felt very well, and we joked about the prosthesis. My colleagues were brilliant and looked after me well. I did experience a bit of nausea, but not enough to interfere with my doing things for myself. At times in the days following my return to work, I got the feeling the other girls were helping me a bit too much, and this made me feel inadequate at times. I sometimes also imagined things that were not there. I became slightly paranoid at times, and I had to take a deep breath to calm myself before entering the ward for my shift.

My prosthesis got stuck while I was at work one, day and one of the ward sisters helped me to get it out. She was so kind, but I did feel embarrassed. My GP reassured me that the prosthesis and the site of the operation were all clean, and she gave me some pain relief. After the week, the pain calmed down, but the prosthesis continued to bug me. Since I had no septum, the prosthesis couldn't sit correctly and shifted around inside the top of my nose quite freely. I felt like a little brat because I didn't like it, but it got stuck again one morning, this time further inside my nose. My husband tried to remove it for me but without success, and I ended up in Accident and Emergency. The A&E doctor pried it out with surgical clamps, as that was the only tool that would work. The procedure took a long time, and I think I screamed the place down the pain was so intense, but the doctor got it out. I never wore the prosthesis again. How do people cope with those things? I admit to being completely ignorant of all these things that become part of life after cancer, as one can never know what others have to suffer as they try to blend in with normal life.

I had not told my children about the cancer immediately; even though they were adults, I did not want to upset them, when I finally told them, they were very angry with me for not saying anything. My youngest girl was furious.

"How dare I keep this from us?" she said. "We are not children anymore."

I was a bit choked up at their reaction; they are very strong kids. I promised them I would never keep things from them again, and they settled down. After that they were worried but very calm about it all. I'm so proud of them. They had already experienced trying times, and my cancer made life harder, but our family bond was strong, and everyone stuck together in this crisis. My children didn't suffocate me but were always there when I needed a hug, and once my treatments began, they stayed by me all the way.

I told my dad about the cancer, but the information didn't seem to register with him; he seems to be getting foggy. I had been his carer for several years at this point, as he had difficulty looking after himself. So my daughter helped me to set him up in a warden-controlled flat, a lovely little place with help at hand for emergencies. He had always been adamant that our family not put him in a home, On Mondays, one of my daughters and I would buy the food he needed for the week, and we cleaned his flat regularly, as he didn't do it. He started to get into difficulties about this time, he also fell down regularly and people were picking him up in the street, on buses, and at home—he even needed stitches in his head after he fell in the wardrobe. As time progressed, he needed more help and his vagueness became more recognisable. He always said to me "please don't put me in a home" which is why we are taking care of him. He had always been a strong, clean, well-dressed man; this man was not the father I knew at all.

Then he hurt his leg badly in a fall, and our family had to get the district nurse in to tend to it. He was increasingly harder for me to look after, especially as he was always calling for me even when I had told him I was going into hospital. My situation just never seemed to register. He used his emergency alarm one day to summon the ambulance to collect his prescription medication, the ambulance crew told me later. I explained that he must never use the alarm for such silly reasons and instead should ask me. So when he fell one day afterwards, instead of using his alarm, he pulled the phone to the floor and rang me. At that point, I said, "Dad, I'm sorry, but you need to go into a residential home. I can't do this anymore." he wasn't happy, but he went anyway. Six weeks later he had a bad turn, and went into hospital the doctors had to amputate his right leg, as he was very ill with sepsis in his leg. I am so glad we moved him into the home; as his primary carer, I would not have been able to cope with such a horrendous injury and treatment, although the amputation did save his life.

Afterwards, my husband took me on holiday to Tenerife so I could get some rest before I started radiotherapy. My daughter, her husband, and their two daughters joined us for a lovely two weeks of relaxation. I love Tenerife. My family visits once a year, and some years twice. Each time I visit, I immediately feel at home. The people are very friendly and appear to be stress-free, and their attitude helps to put me at ease.

Our flight left very early, about 6 a.m., and after arriving and booking in to our hotel, we immediately unpack, and change into summer clothing, out we went. We wandered down to the marina and stopped for a coffee at our favourite café. The waiters all recognised us and welcomed us warmly, I can see them looking at my face because as we had been visiting the place for a few years. I told them a bit warily about my condition, and they gave me a big hug and told me I still look lovely. I smiled; the waiters are such nice people my granddaughters love it there, too, and the waiters spoilt them. I felt so relaxed. It was good to be there.

After coffee, we wandered further down the road to the beach and then paddled as we walked along. Ever since I was a little girl I have loved the sea and paddled as often as I could, as paddling is more fun than just a walking down the promenade.

The next day we hired a car. My husband drove, as I never drive abroad after a trip to France when I went the wrong way around a roundabout. Luckily hardly anyone else was driving then, but the mistake scared the daylights out of my husband, and he's driven on holidays since. In Tenerife, we love to go up the mountains and to the volcano, slowly wandering, stopping a various cafes and shops on the way. As we drove up on this trip, we went right through the clouds. Going up the side of a mountain frightened me, as I felt as though I were going to fall off, but Hubby was used to the drive, so I trusted him completely. It was a bit chilly at the top, so we were glad we had brought jumpers just in case. We then drove into the volcano crater. Wow, what a beautiful sight! So open and so big. We were met by a lot of other cars and coaches, though, so we had difficulty finding a decent parking place.

Once out of the car, we took a cable car to the top of the volcano. Although it was a bit expensive to ride, it was worth doing. Getting into the cable car didn't take long despite the crowds because quite a few people fit in each car. Hubby told me as we rode that when we got to the top, I must not run or walk fast because the air up there is so thin. When we got out at the top I was amazed at the lovely view looking down through the clouds. "It's fantastic!" I said.

After a short time, I start feel a bit light-headed and realised I need to go back down. As I sat waiting for the cable car, I tried to breathe very slowly but was a bit concerned. Thankfully the car arrived before too long, and down we went. I enjoyed the trip, but I won't go up ever again. "Done it once; I won't do it again," I told the family. They just laughed,

On the way back down the mountain, Hubby decided that we should drive down the opposite way we went up, and we all agreed, but once we were off, I wished I had said no. It is a beautiful sight and you definitely need a car to visit this part of the island.

"This isn't a road; it's a dirt path. Get me out of here!" I said. I am such a baby—I do not like unpaved roads like this one. This goes for miles; I saw the road looping up and down and around the mountain for miles below us and totally freaked out. I spent the rest of the ride holding my granddaughters' hands and not looking out the window except to peek as I prayed that we were nearing the end. After nearly two hours, we finally made it back to the motorway, and I quietly breathed a sigh of relief. Despite the fright, this was still a good day out.

The next day, I said that I wanted to see the dolphins and whales, so we bought tickets for a boat trip for the following day. I couldn't wait; I love being out on the sea. The day of the trip, we got up, had breakfast, and then left the hotel to catch a minibus to the boat. The weather was lovely as usual, and I was looking forward to seeing the dolphins at play. The boat stopped in a lovely area below the huge mountains where the sea was so blue and clear. The crew started a waterfall down the back of the boat, and everyone was invited to get in the water to swim. As I dived in, the cold hit me, and I did my best to tense up my nose so it wouldn't fill with water. I just floated on the surface; this was a little bit of heaven. When I returned to the boat, I found lunch waiting. Supplied and served by the crew as part of the day's tour, it was plain, simple, but a very nice meal of chicken and salad. We then returned to the marina and took a minibus back to the hotel. We arrived by 6 p.m., time to have supper and relax in the hotel garden.

The following day, I wanted to swim with the dolphins, so we went to the very pretty park with water flumes for everyone to play in. I paid the entrance fee and flew down the flumes and played in the water while waiting for my turn with the dolphins. I was finally called in at 11 a.m. First, I watched the trainers and listened to the information about these dolphins, including that one of them had just had a baby. Lord, how beautiful they were!

The trainers then took me to kneel in the water, and a dolphin came to me. I stroked her and felt that her skin was smooth and soft. Then I leaned forward, and she kissed me on the lips. The trainers next showed me how to do tricks with the dolphins. In this time and place, I felt so alive and free from all the troubles of the year; the dolphins eased the pain.

After about an hour with the dolphins, I left the trainers to meet up with Hubby and the family, who had stayed behind in another part of the park. Hubby agreed that this was a wonderful day for me; my dreams of being with the dolphins had been fulfilled.

We next went to the dolphin arena area for the daily show and found our reserved seats in the front. As the show went on, I watched my granddaughters' faces and saw such joy that my heart pounded. I'd heard that the trainers usually pick a child from the audience to get a ride around the pool in a boat pulled by the dolphins, and imagine my family's surprise when the trainers chose both of my granddaughters! After the ride, the dolphins gave them kisses. The girls' faces glowed with awe when they came back to our seats; I felt so proud.

Then, imagine my surprise again when one of the trainers asked me to come to the water's edge. He had me sit in the water on a body board, and he held the board behind me as two dolphins pulled us around the pool. If I had laughed and grinned much more, I might have split my face. What a treat! My dream of being with these beautiful creatures really had come true. I loved the experience so much that I cried after it was over. Such a happy time. On the way out of the park later that day, we reviewed all the pictures the staff had taken, which included some of the girls in the boat. My husband asked me which pictures I wanted to purchase, and I laughed and took the lot. They cost a fortune but were so worth it.

The next day we went to Monkey Park at Tenerife Zoo. What a great place where visitors can feed little monkeys from their hands. The weather was very hot, and Hubby insisted I wear the hat I bought after doctors and nurses warned me to protect against sunburn on my face. I never wore hats normally, so I was a bit bratty about it, although I knew wearing it was good for me.

For the rest of the trip, I wanted to explore and do things I had never done before to cross them off my bucket list. One of these was playing sand bowls, organised by the hotel entertainment staff. Now whenever we go there we always try and get a few games in. Such fun. We found lots of different things to do each day. Apart from wandering around, we played in the pool at the hotel, and we sat in the hotel garden almost every night till late watching the amusing entertainment. The stage was close to the pool, and the seating was comfortable enough. A couple of nights we went to dinner down near the marina and the menus looked very appetising. All too soon it was time to go home. I wanted to stay in Tenerife forever. "One day I will retire here," I said. It's nice to have dreams.

CHAPTER 3

Then I went in for radiotherapy. As *NHS Choices* explains, "Radiotherapy, also known as radiation treatment, is the controlled use of high energy X-rays to treat many different types of cancer. About 4 out of 10 people with cancer have radiotherapy. In some cases, radiotherapy can also be used to treat benign (non-cancerous) tumours. The length of each course of radiotherapy will depend on the size and type of cancer and where it is in the body" (http://www.nhs.uk/conditions/Radiotherapy/Pages/Introduction.aspx). The first step for me was to have a mask made. Since the health-care workers called it a *mask*, I expected one that would only go round my face, but no, this one went from head to chest and all around my body, so it clipped to the bed whilst I underwent treatment, keeping me from moving a muscle. As the professionals fitted the mask, they gave me the innards of a syringe to breathe through like a snorkel. There was no room for error as the mask was fitted, especially as I would be given radiation so close to my eyes, although the only side effect of the treatment I was warned about was possibly developing cataracts as I got older. Why is it that a cure must lead to harm as a result?

My husband was shocked as he listened to the explanation of the therapy, as he had done military service in his younger years and had learnt of the dangers of radiation poisoning, and here my body was purposefully being exposed to radiation. He drove me mad with his complaints, and I told him to stop especially after he confronted the oncologist about the treatment. "You're like a bull being shown a red rag," I said. To this day though he still mentions it from time to time, but thankfully not as often as he did during my first treatments, which I received three times a day for the first two and a half weeks.

I was exposed to high-energy X-rays, and because radiologists had to aim the rays very precisely at the exact area of the body to be treated each time, so it was important that I wear the mask to ensure I lay still while the treatment was in progress. My lying still was especially important, as the radiotherapy targeted my head. I only wore the mask during the set-up procedures, which took about fifteen minutes, and during the treatment itself which usually took about ten to fifteen minutes, making the total time I wore the mask approximately thirty minutes for each session.

The oncologist suggested that I stay at the hospital while I underwent treatment, so I stayed at the hospital's lodge for cancer patients and their families, as going home and returning to the hospital every day would have been a chore. It was a nice place: I had my own room with a fridge, kettle, and television in the room and an en suite bathroom, and families shared a joint dining room and living room so they could meet and eat together. Other people undergoing radiotherapy also stayed there with their families, and everyone supported everyone else. The environment was very comfortable and the people very open. Those of us staying at the lodge were free to do as we wished between treatments; most of us went out in the evenings for dinner with our families.

My best friend visited with me for several hours every day while I was between treatments, and sometimes one of her daughters came with her and stayed awhile too. We would wander around and chat mostly about nothing and often go to the hospital restaurant for late breakfast or early lunch. She always made sure I ate and drank plenty. She was my rock during my treatment; I would never have done as well as I did without her there. I spent the evenings with my husband, who would visit and take me out to dinner. He was also my rock.

Each day, I walked over to the treatment rooms with other patients staying at the lodge, as our radiotherapy sessions often coincided. We helped each other through these days, jollying each other along as treatment progressed. I felt fine for the first week and a few days.

The hospital made advisers for people with cancer available at a centre attached to the hospital. These advisers chatted with patients and had coffee with us, and they also led relaxation sessions, which I found so nice. During these sessions, approximately twelve patients would each sit in a recliner and listen to the lady talking, and most of us would simply go off to sleep. Following a session of radiotherapy, I often took advantage of aromatherapy and massages for my feet, back, and head, those offering these treatments were all very helpful, friendly, and professional, and I made some lovely friends during the relaxation treatments. Who are still in contact today I'm pleased to say. We all got together one evening in the second week to have a fish and chip dinner but I was finding the food hard to eat.

By the end of the second week of my treatment my mouth and throat were sore, and, I felt sick and could not eat or drink anything, as I had very painful ulcers in my throat and mouth and on my lips. I was admitted to a ward at the hospital and given a drip, but the radiotherapy continued even with the drip. I didn't want to continue the therapy; I felt washed out, in pain, and miserable, but I forced myself to finish the course.

The radiation had caused the mouth sores and can also lead to infections. This treatment is intended to kill rapidly growing cancer cells, but it also damages some healthy cells in the body as they divide and grow. The radiation also impairs the body's immune system, allowing viruses, bacteria, and fungi to more easily infect the mouth and cause mouth sores. The doctors did tell me that because the radiation targeted my head, I could expect to develop mouth sores, with more intense doses of radiation causing the sores to develop more quickly. Doctors also told me that the sores could last from four to six weeks after the last radiation treatment.

I continued to not eat or drink, and I had even stopped smoking because my mouth felt like it was on fire all the time and if I couldn't eat or drink I knew I definitely couldn't smoke. I was referred to a dietician, who spent time with me, weighed me, and gave me supplement drinks to take whilst I was off food. These supplements came in a variety of flavours, including fruit flavours, and I didn't like them all, but I found I liked the vanilla one because it tasted like ice cream. I couldn't eat properly for several more weeks. "One way to lose weight," I said. I felt I was large enough and could afford to lose plenty of pounds, so the weight loss didn't bother me.

One of the worst things about being in the ward was that I was in a bed about four feet from the bed my mother had been in several years before when she also suffered from cancer, which spread throughout her body over a four-year period. As I lay there, I can see mum in that bed and remembered. She was fifty-six years old, a year older than I am as I write, and a great friend and mother. She developed breast cancer shortly after my younger brother was killed riding his motorbike. She never seemed to get over losing him, although life went on. I believe I can understand how she felt more than I did all those years ago. My brother was five years younger than me, the baby of the family, and very close to our mother. He caused lots of trouble—a typical boy—and his life was cut short in a stupid accident. Life can be very unfair. I suppose that I didn't worry that I would get cancer because, due to my mother's illness, I seemed to know I was destined to get it one day.

The staff looking after me on the ward were lovely and very caring as they helped me through the pain and distress that I felt. They treated my intense pain with fentanyl patches, morphine sulphate tablets (MST), and Oramorph is a liquid version of MST given fairly regularly between doses of the tablets, as it quickly breaks through the pain until the tablets kick in. Fentanyl is prescribed to manage moderate to severe pain, usually to people with chronic pain and often used when other pain medicines no longer work.

I lost my hair underneath at the back of my head as I knew I would, but not a lot, thankfully. I had a large bald patch right the way across my scalp, but unless I lifted the layer of hair above it, the bald patch wasn't noticeable. Each morning when I woke, I found hair on my pillow, and lumps of hair would come away in my hand. The hair loss didn't bother me too much as I expected that it could happen, as it's a common side effect of radiotherapy and would grow back eventually. I joked to family and friends, "How can bald people bear the wind whistling across their scalps?" They found this funny.

I vowed that if the cancer ever came back, I would rather die than be put through radiotherapy treatment again, and I told my family so. I went home after my treatment was over and spent several months sitting in the house. I felt isolated and lonely. Because of all the pills I was on, I spent most of my time in my chair dozing as if I was in a coma. I didn't want to go anywhere or do anything; I had so many pills that I was incapable of doing most chores. I thought, *At least I can't feel the pain now*, but the problem was I didn't feel anything at all. I wondered, *Is this what life is like for my patients? Are they so drugged up that they live in a void?* I wasn't aware of much going on around me. My best friend rang me most days and encouraged me to get out of the house, but I didn't want to.

By the third month, I finally said to myself, "Get rid of the drugs and wake up!" I stopped the pain medication without any further problems and haven't taken morphine since. I went to see my doctor, as I felt tearful because I had not been out of the house prior to this. She referred me to hospice community nurses, who visited patients like me regularly. The nurse who saw me gave me brilliant care and attention. When she came to my house, we chatted for long periods, and I would pour out anything that was in my head and cry a lot. I gradually felt brighter, as getting my feeling out and into perspective, the tears did dry up eventually.

A couple of my work colleagues started to visit me and I even went out to lunch with them a few times. It was a big thing for me and my isolation was definitely of my own doing: I hadn't got much of a nose left, and I felt very self-conscious about it. I hated looking in a mirror, and I'm not generally vain. *What's my problem?* I thought. My best friend kept telling me to get out there, but I couldn't get out even when she was urging me to; I kept imagining people staring at me like I was a freak. Now, looking back, I believe it was all in my head, as I finally summoned the courage to leave the house. *Okay, let's do it,* I thought. I picked up my friend, and we went to bingo. I took a deep breath before I got out of the car, and when we went inside, I looked around as if daring anyone to comment on my appearance, but no one took much notice of me; I received only a few stares. I didn't win that night, though.

By mid-January 2011, I felt ready to go back to work. First I had to see the occupational health team so they could asses my ability to work. When I passed the assessment, I worked with my employer to make a schedule for starting back slowly, with shifts of four hours a days, three days a week until I was healthy enough to handle full-time shifts. My bosses had suggested that I work part-time for the long term, but I felt all right working full-time, as I always say I'm all right. The truth was that I was tired, and although I refused to let it control me, I was back with the occupational health team within two weeks. We then re-started the gradual progression back to full-time work, and I ultimately cut my hours back from 37.5 to 30 hours a week. This time I felt less tired while I was at work, but I was exhausted when I got home. I never admitted it, as I felt it would make me seem weak, and that would never do.

My colleagues all asked me about radiotherapy and wanted to see the mask I had to wear. As I had taken it home but hadn't yet dumped it, I took it into work. My colleagues found it hard to imagine that anyone could wear one of those things, and when I put it on, they asked me to remove it, as they didn't like it at all. I have to laugh a bit now, as they were sincere in their strong feelings about it. When I returned home, I was determined to burn the mask because it was such a horror, but one of my daughters wanted to keep it "for Halloween", she said. I gave it to her, thinking that at least then it wouldn't be at my house, and thankfully I haven't seen it since.

My boss suggested that I might want to think about retirement, but I was only fifty-two; too young for retirement, I thought. I knew my boss meant well and was concerned about my health.

Around this time one of my colleagues at work was also off sick with a cough that didn't seem to clear. She was always a happy soul, and she and I laughed a lot and hugged each other to say hello at the start of our shifts. I hadn't seen her for a while when one day, my boss called all the staff to her office. The ward sisters were both there when we went in, and they seemed to be struggling as they gave us the news that that our sick colleague had been diagnosed with lung cancer. There was nothing that could be done to help her, the sisters explained. The room went quiet. One of the girls burst into tears, and I felt the floor drop out from beneath me. Oh my lord, no!

This colleague passed away two weeks later. How horrible for her family that she was gone so quickly. The ward's morale was low as all the staff grieved for our friend. "Rest in peace, my love," I whispered to myself. I didn't attend her funeral; I felt that I couldn't bear it, and my heart broke because I had just been deemed fit for work. One of the sisters put her arm around me and told me how lucky I had been, and I agreed with her completely.

At this time I was still going back and forth to hospital appointments, and if I wasn't at work, I could be found at some hospital having a check-up. The treatment seemed to never end. I found myself digging back into my hole, as people looked at me or when they spoke to me as if they were speaking only to my nose, and I heard laughs and rude comments here and there. I tried not to let it get to me, but it did. In one instance, a patient's relative came to our ward one day as I was doing the medication round in that area, and he remarked that my face looked like it had been hit by a bus or had I gone a round or two with a boxer, and he chuckled at his comment. I replied that I had cancer and walked away. He never made any comments after that. What was his reasoning or excuse that made him think he could speak to me or to anyone else like that? What is the matter with people? Everyone must learn to think before they speak. I know we all make similar mistakes, but such words hurt so much. Look how many people there are walking around with a disfigurement of some kind, why do people have to be nasty and presume something they know nothing about? A disfigurement can happen to anyone so quickly, and people need to know and understand how it can affect their lives.

Just after going back to work, I went to the stop-smoking clinic at the doctor's surgery, as everyone was telling me I needed to stop, and I knew that, but my mind told me one thing and the rest of me told me something else. I felt so wound up and like everything was closing in on me that I found it hard to cope. My brain wouldn't stop day or night, and insignificant things constantly went through my head. The clinician at the surgery explained the different types of aids used to help people quit. I'd tried patches, acupuncture, and other treatments without success. I just had no willpower. If I didn't need willpower to stop, I wouldn't have a problem not smoking. The counsellor then checked my nicotine levels and sent me home with tablets. I followed the instructions carefully and went back to the stop-smoking clinic two weeks later. My nicotine levels had reduced by half. I was so pleased, but the clinician told me I had to try harder. I went home feeling deflated. Where was the support I was supposed to receive? I thought I had done really well, but the clinician made me feel inadequate. I gave up giving up and never went back to see her. I had more important things to worry about than smoking, and I didn't drink, gamble, or lie. I admit my vice was a bad one, but what was it going to do, give me cancer?

CHAPTER 4

Six months after my radiotherapy, I saw a plastic surgeon to have my nose rebuilt, as most of the left side of my nose was missing. The first step was a CT scan, and I planned to go with a friend, as, strangely, I could drive anywhere except to my hospital appointments. Our routine was to drive to a local station, leave the car, and then get a train into London. On my way to my friend's house, as I'm sitting at a traffic light, the car was suddenly jolted from the rear; someone had hit the back of my car. I couldn't catch my breath, and I felt very shaky. I looked back to see the driver that hit me get out of his large van and come to my driver's side window, he saw that I was shaking;. He suggested we drive to a car park only a few yards away to check my car. There was a lot of traffic on the road, so I agreed, and I vaguely remember pulling into the car park. I took about ten minutes to settle myself down, and then we looked at the damage. His van had suffered no damage. The van driver gave me his name and phone number and said he would pay cash to fix the damage on my car. I agreed, as it didn't look too severe.

Although I was still shaking, I had my appointment to get to, so I then left the other driver and went to collect my friend. I realised my scan was more important than anything that happened to my car, so I settled down.

When I got home, I told my husband about the accident. He was angry and ranted at me a bit. "Why didn't you get his insurance details?"

I don't know, I explained that the other driver had said he'd pay for the damage himself. I think I trust people too much sometimes.

My husband took the car to our local garage, and the mechanics inspected it and determined that the whole underside needed replacing. A thousand pounds to repair the damage, they said.

I rang the driver of the van and told him the estimate. He said he would ring me back in half an hour. Okay, so far so good. An hour later he had not rung, so I rang him again. No answer. I tried several more times to reach him over the next few hours. Still nothing. My husband ranted at me again about having to pay for the repairs on our own. I tried to remember where the crash happened, and I remembered that I was at the traffic lights outside a few businesses, and I went online to find out which businesses they were. I recreated the accident in my mind: the van had come out of one of the businesses' driveways and onto the main road without waiting for a safe space. All I had was the driver's name and phone number, but I guessed that because he was in a van, he must have been making a delivery or doing other business like that. I rang a few of the companies numbers in that area them to see if they recognised the driver's name and got very lucky—one of the managers told me the driver worked for him. I explained the reason for my call, and the manager was not very pleased but told me he would cover the cost of the repairs. My car was taken away the next morning and a courtesy car was left in its place, and the car was repaired in a week.

I then went back to work as usual; no point sitting at home doing nothing. As I was making a bed with a colleague one morning about two weeks later, I felt a pull in my shoulder and then an ache in my neck. I told my colleague, and we just shrugged it off, but as time went on, the pain got worse, so I made an appointment with my doctor, who told me that I had sustained whiplash in the accident. As if things couldn't get any worse! I rang my insurance company, and they arranged for an additional medical exam, and had approximately ten sessions of physiotherapy. The company covered all my claims, but I never heard from the driver again. Why are all these events happening to me? I felt as though I were being punished. I was so fed up.

I was glad that my friend came to my doctors' appointments with me, as she made me feel better by just being there. although it was great when Hubby went with me, and I know he always wanted to be there to support me, but life wouldn't pay for itself and I hadn't been earning much, as I was often off sick from work, so Hubby usually had to work. But I don't intend to be off too long anyway if I can help it.

The results of scans that I had had showed no cancer, and my oncologist declared that I was in remission. If I stayed in remission for five years, I could be declared clear of the cancer.

After eight weeks of being ill from work due to my shoulder, I went back to work again. I had to see the occupational health team, again so they could re-assess my fitness to work. This team were tasked with assessing the impact of work on my health and making sure my health wouldn't cause work-related problems. They were very kind and helpful as we chatted about my illness and treatment. I felt tearful about it all, but I always felt tearful at the time. We then agreed on a new work schedule to ease me back in slowly, as I had been off for a long time, and my bosses were very agreeable to it.

My colleagues welcomed me back lovingly, and I was very lucky to have them. They all supported me and made sure I wasn't overdoing it, but sometimes I felt that they were overdoing the care and time they give me, am I alright?. Am I doing too much, they kept trying to take work from me that I knew I could do, and they made me feel that I couldn't perform adequately.

This made me feel useless. I knew I was imagining this, but I couldn't help it.

On the first day back, I felt very nervous and shaky and lacked confidence. I started my shift as usual, but within three hours, I felt so tired and had to go home. *Dammit! I can't even do three stupid hours*, I thought. I need to do it. So after that I forced myself to work a bit more each day and slowly build up to my full thirty-hour-a-week schedule. I thought I was okay at the end of each day, but when I got home, I had to drag myself out of the car, and once indoors, I sat in my chair and slept till bedtime. This became a habit, but I would never admit I was so tired, as I didn't want to be perceived as a failure. To get myself through the day, I told myself things like, "Don't be pathetic; the treatment is all over. Get to work!" Why is my mind turning me over all the time?

Sometimes I thought God really hated me for some reason, but I didn't know why. My bosses were the best anyone could have, and they genuinely cared about the well-being of members of their staff. They did talk to me a lot, and this embarrassed me sometimes because I felt I was letting the ward down, and I hated to show such weakness, so why am I like this? I hate it. As time went on, some of my confidence returned and things settled down at work, allowing me to get back into my old work habits.

After two more weeks of hospital appointments, my husband and I were off with our two friends to Athens for our yearly long weekend away. The weather was quite cold in Athens, but we didn't mind. We visited all the ruins we could and wandered around shopping, eating, and just relaxing. Athens wasn't bad and the people were friendly, but I wouldn't have wanted to visit for more than a weekend. We arrived home on Sunday, and I was back to work Monday.

A few weeks following, in May, the girls at work arranged a weekend outing on a barge on the Grand Canal, something I had never done before. I was a bit dubious about the trip and was still quite tired, but I thought, why not go? The girls had arranged for us to ride together to cut down the need for everyone to bring a car, which I thought was a great idea, and on the way, those in my car stopped off to buy wine and snacks, and then we met the rest of the crew at a nearby pub for a drink before we started off. The weekend had started already, everyone was in great spirits. One of the bosses was a good captain of the barge, as she had done this sort of boating lots of times before, and the rest of us followed her orders and tried to be good barge hands. My steering left a lot to be desired—in fact, I was useless at it—but I did enjoy it. I learnt how to open and close all the locks. Some of them were hard to move, but we all pitched in. What teamwork! This was great fun but tiring.

One night on the boat I couldn't be bothered to clean out my nose, and when I went to sleep that night, I must have snored very loudly, as I was woken by a pillow thrown at me. My colleagues all laughed and took it in stride, as half my nose was missing, after all. I took it in stride, too, but I did feel embarrassed and apologise for keeping them awake. After that I didn't say anything more about it and neither did my colleagues.

The days on the barge were lovely. The weather was warm, soothing, and peaceful, and as I sat on the roof of the barge, I felt alive again. I didn't know that barges, just like cars, had to stick to the correct side of the canal, but I learnt this on the Saturday. We had gone down a curve when another barge was coming the other way on the wrong side of the canal, and we had to swerve slightly to avoid hitting it, and we ran into some trees. One of the girls had put her pushbike on the roof, and it got caught up in the trees and was being pulled into the canal. Without thinking, I dived onto the roof and grabbed the bike as it went over the side. As I hauled it back on, all of a sudden someone shouted, "Duck!" I moved to duck, but a tree hit me in the head. I held tight to the bike, and luckily I managed to stay on. I tied the bike down and went down to where the other girls were, everyone hooted with laughter. I felt so good; I had regained the strength that I had thought I had lost over the last year.

Each night, we stopped at night and amused ourselves chatting, laughing, drinking, and eating lots of food. We had all brought something from home, so we had a lovely spread. One night one of the girls decided to have a mini disco at about 11 p.m. it was pouring with rain, but we didn't care. We put on our Macs, set up an iPod in the trees, and danced on the bank beside the barge. We got a little wet, but the joking and laughter definitely made up for it.

CHAPTER 5

On Sunday, we got back to the marina and it was time to go home. We all hugged and said goodbye. On the way home, as we neared Windsor Castle, one of the girls said she had never been there, so we turned off to see it. It was quite expensive to get in, so we just looked at the castle from the outside. Then we wandered around the shops, bought some ice cream, and drove down to a local park, How funny today has been as where we played on the swings and the see-saw. I had forgotten how much fun this was, as it had been a long time since I had played in a park. The looks we received from parents accompanying their children made me feel quite naughty. I rang Hubby then and told him where we were and that I would be late getting back. He understood, as he knew I was out with the girls. After two hours of wandering and playing, home we went. What a lovely end to a great weekend.

Life trotted along after that. I still went to hospital for frequent checks. The consultant and his team seem satisfied with my progress, although I told him that I felt very tired. "This is to be expected," they said. "It will pass." My doctors continued to moan about my smoking, as I was still trying to give up but not succeeding.

In August, I felt quite happy, settled, and relaxed, as my family went on holiday in Tenerife for two weeks with my friend and her two daughters, who had never been there. I wanted to give them the best holiday ever and suggested that my friend should go for a swim with the dolphins. She had been feeling down prior to the holiday, she and loves dolphins as much as I do, so I thought it would be just the thing to make her feel better. She agreed and took her girls with her as whilst Hubby and I went off on our own for a few hours. When we all met up again afterwards, my friend was positively glowing. I was so pleased. I think everyone should experience this type of therapy, as I call it.

After that, Hubby and I showed off the island to my friend and her girls by doing all the things we usually liked to do. Tenerife always feels like home when we visit, and I felt proud that our guests loved it to. We spent a lot of time in the sea on this trip, which I loved. Hubby is not a lover of sitting on the beach, so I was glad to have the chance to be at the seaside for a change. We seemed to do nothing but chat and laugh. My friend's daughters are such lovely girls and did and said such funny things. This was a great holiday, but all too soon, the holiday was over and we had to go home.

I returned to work and more operations. I still felt so tired at the end of each day; nothing seemed to have changed.

Not long after, I started buying the Christmas presents. Hubby came shopping with me, as he does every year. We love to buy presents, even if they're just silly things, and we have fun as we shop. I was scheduled to work through part of the Christmas period, but I had a pretty good shift that year, so I was happy with it.

On New Year's Eve 2012, I was told to go straight to my daughter's house for a party after I came home from work at 9.30 p.m. I couldn't be bothered to go home and change, as I'd had a long busy shift at work and felt tired, so I went straight to her house from work. Everyone was there and in good spirits. My youngest girl still suffered from headaches but looked fantastic. Her weight was down since the steroid treatment. Her advice was that if you want to be thinner, then you must work on it. She had no patience for those overweight people who moaned about their size but didn't try to do anything about it, she does get some funny ideas in her head.

I greeted all my family members and friends, and my eldest daughter gave me a hug. "Hi, Mum. I'm pregnant," she whispered. My goodness! I hugged her hard. What a fantastic present for New Year's! This was her third try.

She laughed and said, "You're crying."

"No I'm not," I said, but I was a little. Really, I was so happy for her.

By now the house was getting very crowded with all our friends everyone is in fancy dress. They all looked great. As we saw the New Year in, I went around and got many hugs, and then we had a drink to toast New Year. Soon after that, I said to Hubby, "I'm tired and would like to go home." He looked at me a bit worriedly, but I assured him I was just tired, so he left with me, no questions asked. I enjoyed myself; I think I was glowing when I learnt I was going to be a grandma again.

By this time I had had five or six operations with the plastic surgeons' but I was still going between work and operations. These operations were done very expertly, as the surgeons said the nose was probably the hardest to rebuild when nothing was left inside. First the surgeon took skin flaps from my forehead to make the outer skin of my nose, and then he had to think of rebuilding the bone and cartilage. He took cartilage from my rib, so I now have a scar along the underside of my left breast, but unfortunately that graft did not take shape and had to be removed. The surgeon then used a part of my skull for the graft, leaving me with a scar hidden in my hair down the left side of my head. I still suffered headaches from time to time, but because of the operations, my head was mostly numb. It was weird to rub the top of my head but feel nothing, but this wasn't harmful, and I didn't feel much pain after the operations.

Before each operation, I didn't think about what was going to happen; I just shut my eyes and let the surgeons get on with it. And I didn't like looking in the mirror much, as I thought I looked a bit like Frankenstein's monster, but I can laugh at the idea and do tell people about my feelings when they ask. I am not a vain person but still don't like the look of my face. People still told me that I looked good, I do smile and say thank you but well I'm sorry, but I didn't agree.

As I went in for another operation, the surgeon rushed me back to the theatre, as the skin graft from my head had become black and necrotic, meaning that the cells had died. After the second operation that week, when the surgeon came in to see me, he slammed his folders on my bed and accused me of not looking after my face, and because I was still smoking, he said I was responsible for the failure of the graft. When he left, I was in tears and rang home to tell my husband about it. He was furious that the surgeon could be so insensitive to me, and he complained to the hospital.

The following day the surgeon came to my bed with the ward sister and apologised to me. He said he hadn't meant to upset me so. We then chatted and agreed that for the most part, the problem was, in fact, caused by the intensity of the radiotherapy I had undergone and not necessarily caused by my smoking—the radiotherapy had actually burnt all the cells in my face, leaving it half dead inside. He and I agreed to leave any more disagreements behind us and carry on.

I was crying hysterically by this time, and the ward sister sat with me and asked me what I was feeling.

"I don't know," I said. "I'm sorry I'm upsetting my treatment."

She told me I had nothing to be sorry for and then asked if there something more I wanted to say,

I just blurted out, "I'm sorry to not be at home or work where I'm needed; I'm sorry I have cancer; I'm sorry!" I put my hand to my mouth and looked at the sister in shock. What was I saying? What was I doing? I couldn't bear this, but I had to or that would be the end, I thought. I felt so small and lonely and scarred inside and out from the radiotherapy. I was so tired I couldn't think anymore, and I felt like I was just going through the motions of life. But I had to be strong,

I reminded myself, because I'm sure that was what everyone wanted.

Tomorrow I can go home, I thought, where everything is normal. *I won't tell Hubby about my conversation at the hospital. Why should I? I need to just leave it and not over-react.*

Hubby had been trying so hard to please me and to help me, but I hadn't been in the best of moods lately, and he had told me that he didn't know what to do. "No matter what I do, you don't appear to be happy with it," he said. But I told him he could stop trying so hard. I loved him and appreciated everything, I went on, but this didn't seem to get through to him. He still seemed to think that he was failing me when he wasn't.

Then it was St Patrick's Day, the day of my second eldest child's wedding. It was wet and sunny all at the same time. I felt a bit peeved because the operations should have been finished by then, as the surgeon had told me he would try to do, but that hadn't wasn't happened, and I was left to make the best of a bad situation. I dreaded the wedding because my face was not a pretty picture, but away I went. *Keep quiet and carry on*, I told myself yet again. Between work, organising the wedding, operations, and life at home, the last few months had been busy, and I hadn't really thought much about my face. Being busy was good for me because it helped me to forget all the other problems I had.

First thing in the morning on the day of the wedding, my hubby, some of the family, friends and I rushed down to the reception site to decorate the whole hall. I felt very fussy and panicky, as I had never taken on such a task before. Hubby and one of our friends worked to get the balloons up whilst my niece and I started on the tables. The photographer then arrived to photo what we were doing, and I roped him into helping us lay tables between taking pictures. The tables didn't require much work, just some prettying up with balloons and favours, because the wedding was a buffet affair. After about two hours, the hall looked good. I felt very proud and very tired.

On the way back home, I had to stop at the baker's for French sticks, as I wanted them to be fresh that day, and a friend took charge of them when I got home. The house was bedlam: all five bridesmaids were there, as was the hairdresser, my next door neighbours. She was great, we gave her a lot to do in such a little time, she has only two hours, but she wasn't fazed, and the girls' hair looked lovely. The bridesmaids did each other's make-up when they weren't having their hair styled. Everyone was in good spirits and having fun, and I was really pleased everything had gone well so far. One of my daughters told me to sit, and she straightened my frizzy hair whilst another put make-up on me—just a little foundation to try to cover my scars. Although she did her best, the scars still showed, but I made the best of it.

When everyone was ready, the car arrived, and off we all went. We were a bit worried that it had been raining all morning, but by the time we got to the church, the rain had stopped. Hubby, my niece, and I had worked very hard to decorate the church and the reception hall. The bride wanted balloon arches, so Hubby and I looked at having decorator coming in, but the prices were over the top, so we did it ourselves. We spent time looking around and getting ideas for decorating a function hall. My clever hubby and one of our dear friends made the balloon arches, and we managed to achieve just about everything else my daughter wanted as well. We had spent a lot of time shopping for the supplies we needed, and we made sure everything was very tasteful and followed the lemon-and-white colour scheme. The hall looked great.

I also served as caterer, and my family helped me with the food. It took six hours to prepare and cook everything, and we worked through half the night, but we had a lot of fun doing it. What a great time we all had. I am very lucky and so grateful for the people in my life. They're all so loving, caring, and giving most of the time. After the ceremony, a friend and her husband rushed off to my house to collect all the food trays and take them to the reception hall, and by the time I arrived, they had everything laid out and ready. They did a wonderful job, and I'm very grateful to them. The wedding was lovely.

The photographer took lots of pictures at the church and at the reception. I made sure that I was not in many of them, as I felt quite nervy. My nose looked horrid. Everyone said how well I looked and nice, I know they are being very kind but they don't see what I see in the mirror each day.

The reception went very well. The guests had lots to eat, the disco was fun, and everyone appeared to be enjoying themselves. There was not a lot of food left after the party, so we knew all was well. I spent most of the time at the reception chatting with people and generally checking that all was well with the guests. Everyone told me what a lovely wedding this was. When I finally sat with my family, I heaved a sigh of relief. I had done my part, but the work was over, and I could finally relax. But not for long.

My friend's hubby rang me the next morning. "She's had a little heart attack," he said. I dropped everything and drove straight to the hospital. I was glad to find her up and about, but she was so pale. We sat and chatted a while until she had to go off for tests. Then her hubby and I decided to go to the hospital restaurant for some lunch. I was so relieved that my friend seemed all right, but she had got a warning, and I was scared. I did not want to lose her, too. Life was really getting on my nerves. After lunch, my friend's hubby and I waited in the ward for my friend to come back. When she did, she told me that the heart attack had scared her and that she was going to be careful from now on. As I drove home that afternoon, I sighed. *Thank God she is okay*, I thought.

CHAPTER 6

In May 2012, I took a week off work to baby-sit my granddaughters whilst their mum and dad went on their honeymoon. I found it funny that people now seemed to want to make a home first, and then have children, and then get married, I do laugh at it, things are all back to front. My mum would have murdered me if I had started my life like that, but all is good and times have changed.

Goodness, what a busy week I had getting my granddaughters ready each day, taking the little love to school and seeing the older love off to her bus, collecting the little one from school, making supper, getting the girls bathed, playing till bedtime, and then getting up in the morning to do it all again. My granddaughters were such good girls, though, and I did love having them. By the end of the week, I believe a treat was in order for them, so we went off to Harvester for a meal, just the three of us. We laughed a lot. I took pictures of them on my phone with their drinks and very large ice creams and sent the pictures to their mum and dad to show them they were having fun with me.

After lunch we went to the Harry Potter museum. Watching the joy on my granddaughters' faces gave my heart such joy. I love being a grandmother. My granddaughters are so precious to me, and I love them so much. I love the cuddles and hugs they give me.

When the newlyweds returned home at the end of the week, I was shattered even though it was lovely to have the little girls for the week. And then I went back to work for a rest, but the rest didn't last long, as at the end of the month, I was off to Dartmouth with my best friend and our hubbies. She is feeling better and had rested the last few weeks after her heart attack and was looking forward to the holiday.

We had planned the trip for months and decided to leave at about 6 a.m. to avoid some of the motorway traffic, planning to have breakfast on the way if we reached a good place at a good time, and that is what we did. We then took our time on the rest of the journey, stopping for drinks and toilet breaks on the way. We had got a weather warning earlier in the week, and the rain came down much more heavily as the day went on, but we had all day, so we didn't mind. Then, what a laugh we had when we got stuck in traffic on the border of Devon because of flooding. But we did get a weather warning earlier in the week but it didn't seem that bad, hubby had his window open as he smoked a cigarette, and I sat behind him, when whoosh! A car passed us, sending water from the road straight into the car like a tidal wave, totally drenching hubby and me. This got the week off to a fun, but unexpected, start.

Our chalet in Dartmouth was just big enough for four people, with two bedrooms and a very small kitchen. The place was fairly clean but dusty from being unoccupied, so we tidied up a little and then went to the local store for groceries. One bedroom had a double bed, and the other had a single bed and a set of bunks. My hubby and I got the bunks and single bed. The mattresses were very lumpy, and I couldn't sleep. I had to get up in the night, as my back was killing me, and I went into the living room to read. The armchair was a comfortable as the beds; this was not good.

During the first part of the week, we went sightseeing, first on a boat ride down to a castle with some lovely sights. We wandered the area and walked through the woods on this nice day which wasn't very warm but was bearable. At lunchtime we decided to have cream tea. I loved the scones, as they were warm, soft, and very tasty. We then spent the evening in the chalet. The men had a few beers, and we all chatted for a long time. I was dreading going to bed after the night I had had, so my friends suggested that I put a sleeping bag under the sheet for more padding. *Why not?* I thought. I followed her advice and slept better but still didn't sleep through the whole night, and I still had a backache in the morning, although not as bad as before.

The next morning we took the ferry to Torquay. It was very nice there and we wandered around the shops and bought some little presents to take back for the kids. Something was bugging my friend. I didn't know what, it was but I sensed there was going to be problems ahead. I was a bit worried about her because of her recent heart attack.

Halfway through the week, everything seemed all right as we shopped in the town. My friend said she was going to the public toilets, so the rest of us said we would wait in the street where we were. After a while we started to wonder where she was and looked for her. As I looked over to the marina, I saw her sitting on a bench with her back to us. The men and I went to join her. We wondered why she had not come back to join us, and she never said a word. In fact, she had stopped talking to us altogether. I had no idea why.

We then went to Bygones in Torquay for a day trip. I was feeling a bit peeved, as my friend still did not talk to us. She was quiet when we went into the cafe for coffees. We had finished looking around and we went from there to visit some caves I had wanted to see, but my friend's husband didn't want to go in because he had been there before, and he seemed angry that we had gone there. Again I didn't understand why. My husband said we would go in because I have never been in and I still really wanted to go in, so my husband and I went and our friends waited in the cafe attached to the entrance.

When we came out of the caves, my friend suggested we get a fish-and-chip supper, and the rest of us agreed. However, when we got back to Dartmouth and found the fish-and-chip booth, my friend passed it by and went into the restaurant. I looked at the menu, thinking maybe she had simply changed her mind, but then I saw the prices and said I was not paying this amount for fish and chips in the restaurant and preferred to go to the booth. My friend seemed to glare at me. I didn't know why.

By this time I felt very tired, as I had not had a lot of sleep, and my back ached badly, so I said, "You know what? I think I want to go home."

"Right, then she said. "We will go now," and she marched out of the restaurant. I looked at my hubby, who just shrugged, and he and I followed my friend and her husband out. Back at the chalet, no one talked as we packed. This was silly, really. My husband had been driving around all day and now had to face four to five more hours of driving to reach home, and my friend did not usually forget that he might be tired. When I mentioned all the driving to my husband, he said, "Let's just get home." So we headed home two days early.

The tension in the car was horrid as we drove in silence, but I wouldn't speak I just sat quietly all the way home, my friend did the same. Would I ever know what was going through her mind? I didn't know and probably didn't want to know. We dropped our friends off at their house without a goodbye, and I haven't seen my friend since. I think I was upset more than anything because we had broken our friendship about ten years before for about three months because of outside influence, and we vowed after we made up that we would always talk and that nothing would come between us again. She appeared to have forgotten that vow, but I hadn't. I thought of her a lot and wondered if she was all right. I still loved her very much but wouldn't go to speak with her. *I can't*, I told myself, and she was clearly of the same mind. We both can be very bloody-minded and we haven't spoken since.

CHAPTER 7

In August 2012, my family were off to a music festival that we'd been going to every year since my children were very young, now and my grandchildren love the festival too. I hadn't gone for two years because of the cancer. I was too tired, and camping was not something I relished doing, as the worry of getting a cold during treatment was too much. But this year, even though I was still having operations, I felt so well, and we would soon be busy with our new grandchild, so I wanted to attend.

The days were sunny and warm but the nights were very cold, but we only had to endure them from Thursday to Sunday. The music was lovely as usual, and we loved to wander around the village, walk along the canal, and stop for a beer at the cricket club, where all the festival-goers were congregated just stretched out on the grass, laughing, and chatting. The weekend was relaxing but sad, too, as my friend who had gone with us to Dartmouth and her husband usually came to the festival with us, but as I have not seen her and we still weren't talking to each other. The festival wasn't the same without her. On Saturday night, as we made our way back to the tent, my daughter rang. "Mum,

I'm off to the hospital," she said. I had promised to be there at the birth, so my husband, our friend, my son, and I rushed to take down the tent and quickly and shoved all our gear in the boot of the car! I was very excited by this point and drove home, and we arrived at 2.30 a.m. My daughter rang then to tell us that the hospital had sent her home. Oh well. We were all so tired that we just went to bed.

At about eight the next morning, my daughter rang again to say she was on the way back to the hospital. "Okay," I said, "I will meet you there."

I arrived at the hospital to find that my daughter was receiving fantastic support from her partner and his mother, and I was glad that they were such good friends and made a lovely addition to our family. The hospital staff allowed my daughter's partner and one other person to be with my daughter, so her partner's mum and I took turns in the room during my daughter's labour, with a joint agreement that when the time came for the baby to be born, I would be in the room. A few hours later, my new grandchild came. Goodness, a BOY! We have not had a boy in the family for the last 23 years since the birth of my son. He was so beautiful that I had to shout it. I felt honoured to have been there at his birth. I had a week off afterwards, and then I went back to work, but only for three weeks before we were off on holiday again. At least I didn't have to work much that month.

When September came, my husband and I and two of my friends were off to Tenerife again. My friends had been there before but had never travelled around the island. They flew out of a different airport and were ten minutes behind my husband and me, so we waited outside in the sun for their flight to arrive.

My friend had told me the day before to make sure I was well shaved for the beach, and we laughed. She and I chat about lots of daft things. I told her that I would plait my armpits just for her. "Don't you dare!" she said, but that evening, I went round to my daughter's house and borrowed my granddaughter's little pink plaited hairpieces. When I arrived at the airport in Tenerife, I tucked them into the sleeves of my T-shirt and waited.

When our friends arrived, I gave them a big hug, and then the friend I had spoken to on the phone saw my arms and burst out laughing. I just looked at her innocently at her and grinned. "You nutter!" she said.

We then got a taxi to the hotel as usual. We never take the tour bus from the airport, as it takes ages to get to the hotels and we are not lovers of coaches. Once we got booked into our rooms, we went to the town to get bits we thought we might need and then wandered, just enjoying and soaking in the sun, a good start of our holiday. As we had done before, we walked along the beach, paddling as we went, instead of walking down the streets since I love the sea so much. When Mum and Dad took my brothers and me to the seaside on holidays, we kids would think nothing of rushing into the water fully dressed.

My husband and I hired a car for four days so we could take our friends on a tour around the island. We needed a car to see all the beautiful sights, as tour buses took forever and were so cramped and uncomfortable.

During the two weeks in Tenerife, we shopped a lot, walked along the coast, and tried out local foods. We also relaxed on the beach a lot under umbrellas and on the beds we had hired. Mmm, lovely. The bars were only about fifty yards from our spot on the beach, so Hubby and our friends went to a bar one particular day. I napped on my sun bed whilst waiting, but when they hadn't come back after about two hours, I was beginning to get a bit peeved. I was very hot and thirsty and needed the toilet.

When they finally returned, I snapped at my husband, "Selfish! You left me here all this time alone." I tried to say it jokingly because I didn't want to get into a tangle with him.

"We watched the football there," Hubby said, and then I really felt mad, as he is a rugby lover and never watches football on television at our house, "You don't watch football "I told him.

"I know, but we were having a beer and just started watching the game."

I was not happy, but I gave up as usual to keep the peace. It wasn't worth ruining the rest of my holiday over football, but I was seething inside.

Towards the end of the first week, my husband and I bought our friends a body board, as they loved to play in the waves, and we all had a go. What fun this was! Because of the tides, the waves shifted at certain times of the day, so we spent some of our time just trying to stand up but getting half drowned by the waves.

As I always do in Tenerife, I felt at home. I've said often that I want to retire there, and you never know, it might just happen. It's nice to have dreams.

When we got home from our holiday, I waited for my next operation to be scheduled. I hadn't heard a thing from the hospital, so I rang the secretary, who told me that the surgeon would see me again when I had stopped smoking. I was quite agitated by this time, and unfortunately, the agitation and being ordered to stop made me want to smoke all the more, especially when you are told "YOU WILL stop". I'd had enough. I emailed the hospital's patient liaison office

(PALS), who offer confidential advice, support, and information on health-related matters to patients, their families, and their carers, because I knew I wouldn't get to speak to the surgeon directly. I stated that if the surgeon wouldn't carry on with the surgeries because of my bad habit, then we would part company. I knew people out there with much worse habits than my smoking had had successful plastic surgeries. The PALS officers contacted the surgeon and then emailed me to remind me that I was booked in for an operation that month. I responded by thanking them but also stating that I had known nothing about being booked in for another operation as yet. Two days later, a letter arrived to inform me of my booking as an inpatient. I truly believe that if I had not contacted PALS, the operation would not have been booked and the letter wouldn't have arrived.

However, I had told my bosses that the operations were done as far as I was concerned. I was fed up with it all. Every time I had an operation, I was able to convince myself to overcome my nerves by shutting my eyes and letting the surgeon get on with his work, but the sparring with the doctor in between operations had gotten to me. I had asked in a letter whether I received bad attitudes because I wasn't a private patient, but I was assured that that wasn't the reason, and my impression of the situation may have just been my imagination running riot, as usual.

After I received the letter, I went to see my manager to tell her that I was, in fact, carrying on with the plastic surgery. I had changed my mind again; I wasn't sure why. What was the matter with me? Why am I putting myself in this position? Operation after operation. Then, in November, I was back in hospital. Fingers crossed.

The surgeon took another skin flap from my forehead and attached it down the side of my nose. Afterwards, I remember thinking that I looked like the elephant man. According to Wikipedia, this type of surgery, called flap surgery, "is a technique used in plastic and reconstructive surgery where any type of tissue is lifted from a donor site and moved to a recipient site with an intact blood supply.... This is done to fill a defect such as a wound resulting from injury or surgery when the remaining tissue is unable to support a graft, or to rebuild more complex anatomic structures", such as my face (http://en.wikipedia.org/wiki/Flap_(surgery)).

I didn't go out after the surgery. Apart from the fact that it was very cold out and I didn't like how I looked, I needed to look after the site of my surgery, as anything could have gone wrong with it. Two weeks later, I hadn't smoked and went back to the hospital for a check up. I felt very proud of myself. But then, I didn't know what happened, but in the days following I was so agitated, and out came a cigarette. I spend several days after swearing at myself in my head. *I'm so stupid. Why can't I stop smoking?* I thought. I'd tried patches, inhalers, you name, but still I couldn't stop. My brain worked overtime and I couldn't sleep. With only two to three hours in bed if I was lucky, I'm getting very tired, and my sleep pattern was disrupted. I would drop off in my chair at the drop of a hat. I didn't saying anything to my family about it because I didn't want to worry them. I had to put up a good front to prove to myself and everyone else that I could do anything.

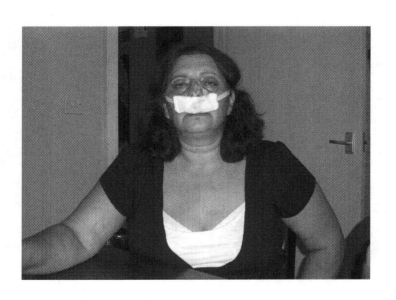

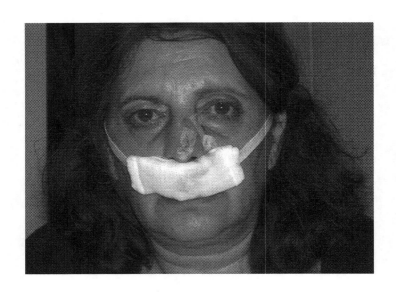

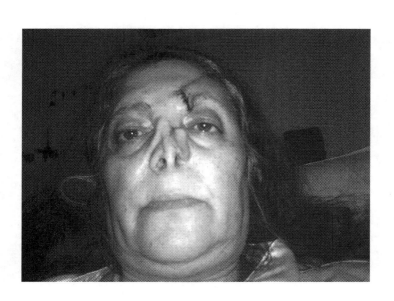

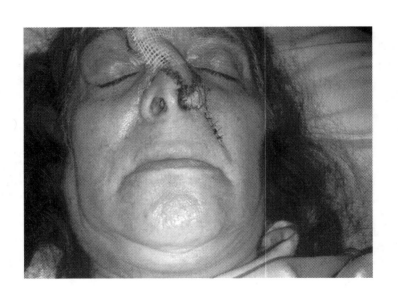

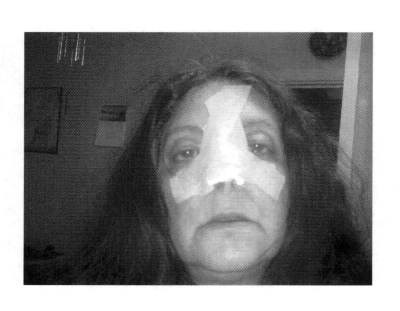

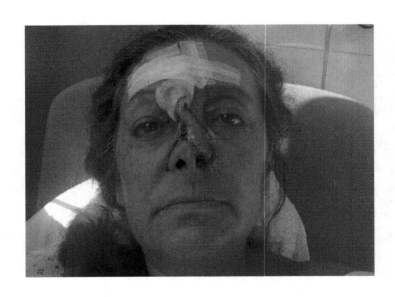

CHAPTER 8

In January 2013, I was in hospital again having more surgery to straighten my face, which had already undergone several changes: They had taken a section of rib cartridge to form a bridge to rebuild my nose after the piece of rib used to make the nose didn't take they removed some portion of skull bone and screwed it in: This has worked well and I could see a nose forming. Still, I am getting a bit fed up, with the scars, and as time went on, I had a harder time dealing with them.

During this hospital stay, the heating on the ward wasn't working properly, and my blood pressure and temperature dropped. The doctor was called to the ward, and after giving me a check-up, he ordered a 'bear hugger' from the theatre to keep my body temperature up, he also prescribed oxygen as my saturation levels were low. All this extended my stay in hospital for an extra week, the doctor said that because it was snowing outside I would be better off in hospital. I didn't argue because I knew he was right and I didn't feel too well, also and I also don't smoke whilst in hospital, so that was a bonus.

After I returned home, I began feeling excessively tired and got quite weepy. I chatted with my husband, my boss, and my GP and then made the decision to retire under ill health, although I still felt too young at only fifty-four. *What I am doing?* I thought. *I'm wearing myself down.* I wondered why I had let myself become like this and thought that maybe I should have made some changes to my life over the last few years Maybe I should have slowed down a bit, as my boss had suggested, but I believed my fatigue would disappear as I worked through all my heartache. I'm not overly strong but I'm not a weakling either, but one can only take so much, and eventually the time comes to say that's enough.

I feel odd at the moment, not odd as in unwell, as I felt quite well, but sad. Sometimes I didn't know what to do with myself. I wanted to contact my oldest friend, but we still weren't speaking, and my pride got in the way. She wouldn't contact me either. Things were going around in my head since I made the decision to retire. *Am I doing the right thing? Then I say to myself of course I am. My body needs to become stronger.* In all the years since my diagnosis, I have just got on with it, because if I don't think about it my illnesses would go away, as I told myself they weren't real, so I have kept myself busy working. But when I look back I see that I was avoiding what I should have faced.

Everyone kept telling me how brave I was. I wasn't brave. I was just choosing to ignore the obvious.

At the end of February, I was sitting at home having had yet another operation. I couldn't go out because it was cold and still snowing, and the doctors wanted me to keep warm. I tried to do housework in between resting, as I was fed up with resting. I have not seen many people around this time. Family members came often to visit, but I was isolating myself again, as I'm a bit nervous about healing properly, this time as I hoped I had had the last big operation on my nose. I decided I wouldn't have another surgery if this graft also failed, but my mind was running around in circles as usual, and I knew I'd probably change my mind again.

In the next few days, I have been getting a pain in my right hip that made walking difficult. I knew what the problem was: I hadn't been running around like usual; I wasn't used to being inactive. I tried to move around, take hot baths, and anything to move the joint and relieve the pain. On my niece's birthday, my husband and I had invited everyone to our house for a dinner party, as I couldn't go out. Everyone knew my hip was hurting and helped out with the preparations.

My youngest daughter insisted on cooking. "Just sit down, Mum," she said. "I'm doing it today. You just relax." So I sat and chatted with her while she cooked, she and all my children are good to me; I'm very lucky.

After about half an hour, my daughter went out of the kitchen for a few minutes, so because I just cannot resist it I decided to get up and do something, as it's not in my nature to just sit around. But as I stood up, oh my Lord the pain in my hip was bad, and I actually screamed. The family all came running into the kitchen, telling me to sit and asking what was wrong.

After about ten minutes, the pain subsided and I was able to relax again. I don't move again; I was too scared to. This pain was another thing I didn't need in my life, why life is so frustrating right now I laugh and just say "I'm falling to bits," I told the family, but they were not amused. I've found joking to be a good way to gloss over my problems, but sometimes I do it at the wrong times. I kept quiet after that.

Not long after, my daughter came over with my little grandson, who was six months old by then and on the move. He was so beautiful, and I my heart was filled with love. My daughter and I put a cover on the floor and set him on it with some toys, and he just rolls everywhere. How quickly children grow, and how proud I am of my family.

After that, on a Monday morning, I was off to the hospital. I did not have to book in till twelve, so my husband and I took our time. When we arrived, I was quite surprised that so few people were there. I guessed everyone else were on the morning lists.

Within ten minutes, I was called in to have my blood pressure checked and to be prepped for theatre. The area where I waited was a bit strange, because men and women sat around wearing surgical gowns. When I was called to the theatre at 2 p.m., a nurse walked with me to the lift and led me to the anaesthetics room on the top floor. The doctors and nurses there were very nice and put me at ease for a while. They told me when it was time for me to sleep, so I took a breath to relax myself and push away the dread I always felt at this point and waited to fall asleep.

I woke at about 3 p.m. The nurse looking after me had a few other patients as well and was very nice but very busy. She left me to doze and to wake up properly, which was nice for me, but at 5 p.m., she told me that the bed allocated for me in a ward still wasn't vacant. At 7 p.m. the bed still wasn't vacant. I asked the nurse to ring my husband so I could go home instead, but she said without permission from a doctor, that wasn't ideal. I said I was happy to discharge myself, as if there wasn't a bed, I really did not want to stay any longer. By now I had gone over the four-hour limit on a theatre trolley and my bottom was feeling very sore. The pressure was getting very uncomfortable. The nurse made me a coffee and asked me to wait a bit longer. I agreed but wasn't overly happy. Another patient, a man, was now wandering around the recovery area in his gown, and I think he was fed up too. Finally, at about 8 p.m., I got to the ward. The staff were just changing for the night shift. This was a very long day after all. *Why doesn't anything ever go right?*

I had a check-up, including a blood pressure check, and then I tried and go to sleep, but pain woke me up about every two hours. I needed some pain relief by 4 a.m., the nurses were happy to oblige me with pills and a cup of coffee. The staff in this ward were lovely and looked after me well. I usually came here after my surgeries, so we had got to know each other by now. In the morning, the team came to see me on their ward round and discharged me. Before going home, I set an appointment for a follow-up in the outpatient's department, and then, after a few weeks, I'd have another tidy-up on my nose in the hospital.

Three days later I had been in a bit of pain in my head, the stitches felt a bit tight, so I would sit and massage my head. It's also become a bit itchy all over and my forehead and the top of my head perhaps because of the numbness in my face that I've had since the beginning of the major operations. It's an odd feeling to not be able to feel your head, and I felt something was writhing around in my head, hence the itchiness, I scratched an awful lot though. I asked the doctor about it at my check-up that day, and he didn't seem too concerned and said he was pleased with the results so far. He also said that I had maybe two more operations to go before we are done. I hoped so.

The next day my husband and I went to Reading to stay overnight with friends. I had been looking forward to the visit with these lovely friends. We arrived at about 1 p.m. to a warm welcome, and I relaxed nicely. We had planned to go out to lunch, but my friend likes to cook and gave me the choice to stay in instead. As she was such a great cook, I opted to stay in. Afterwards she and I left the men behind for a while and went for a bit of retail therapy in her new car. I thought this would be a good outing. At the shops, I couldn't really find anything I wanted, so we went for a treat of a cream tea with all the trimmings. Yum! Scones with jam and Cornish cream, they were my favourite. We then headed back home. The road system in Reading was a bit odd, and because of all the roadworks, we had to go out of the area completely. We laughed about it and had a lovely ride through the countryside, although we had no idea where we were but who cares its fun. We eventually got back about an hour or so later very happy and relaxed. While we were out, the men watched a film, but they didn't seem to have even noticed how long we were. We all had a good laugh about that 'men' I don't know. It's nice to leave them to their own devices at times.

After a great dinner, we settled on playing a music trivia game on the PlayStation. My friends and I were useless, but my hubby, being a musician, seemed to know all the answers and raced off in front of us. "Show-off," I said. He just gave me a blank look. "What?" he said. What a laugh we had! Before we knew it, it was 1 a.m., time for bed. I slept very well for a change. I think relaxing really helped.

In the morning we had a full breakfast and then headed home. I have felt totally pampered and spoilt this weekend, as I always do when we visit these friends. They are my granddaughter's godparents, and the husbands' mum was my godmother, so we have always regarded each other as family, and I do love them very much. When we got home, I sat and nodded off for a while, although it was great I still felt worn out. But that night I got to bed at a reasonable time and woke up the next morning feeling quite well.

We got back into the normal grind after that. By this time I had been off work almost three months. I did get the occasional call and saw my children and grandchildren regularly, but I was mostly back in isolation again, probably by my own doing. I had found that a long-term illness made me realise what was truly important to me. After the novelty of the illness had worn off, I realised that life had to go on regardless of how I felt. I don't expect people to run around after me, and I never had, but sometimes I did feel lonely. Is this how my patients feel? Or is this my doing. ?

Sometimes I found myself apologising to various people because I believed either that I was letting them down or that I had upset them in some way, and sometimes I apologised just for being ill. *It's not my fault!* I shouted at myself. I did not ask for bloody cancer. But I refused to let it get me down and realised I needed to get my life together in another way, and change things around to suit what I felt up to doing.

At one point I went out for an hour with my son today to play badminton, something we've done together since he was a little boy. We had a good laugh at how rubbish we were, but I did enjoy it. Afterwards I felt a bit tired and heady, but not too bad.

That same day, I had agreed to care for my two granddaughters overnight. I picked up the younger one from school at 3.15 p.m. When she came out of class, she saw me and shouted, "Nanny!" and ran straight into me. What a lovely welcome. She does this all the time and always makes me feel very loved.

When we got home, she wanted to bake, so I told her we'd do some baking in the morning and I had already bought everything we needed. My older granddaughter then arrived at 4 p.m. After supper, we settled in to watch a film, and then I bathed the little one, a task that was always a laugh. I didn't leave her alone in the bath as she's only seven, so I usually got very wet, and the bathroom floor looked like a paddling pool when we were finished. After a bit of playtime, it was nearly 10 p.m. The girls moaned because they didn't want to go to bed, but I reminded them that it was very late now. I didn't mind that they went to bed so late, as it was Friday and they could sleep in on Saturday.

They next morning, the girls had breakfast and then the baking started. By lunchtime we had made Easter cookies, cupcakes, and a marble cake, and quite a mess with the flour everywhere, but it was fun, and it reminded me of cooking with my children when they were young. My younger granddaughter was a bit moody and wanted to cook alone with me and not with her sister, but I said, "No, we'll all do it together." The younger girl's favourite bit is licking the spoons and bowls when we are done. This time there was a lot of batter left over, and I had to keep her from having too much. That was enough cooking for the day, as I was starting to feel a bit worn out.

My daughter arrived at about 1 p.m., and off my grandchildren went to the cinema with Mum and Dad. Although I love having them stay with me, it was a relief after they left because all I wanted to do was rest.

I got a call a little later from my daughter, who told me that the little one had eaten too much and had vomited during the film, so they had to go home and miss most of it. Three times my daughter said, "I think there's more to it." Oh dear, I thought. This was my fault because I had let her lick the bowls clean after baking.

I was alone that night, as Hubby worked the night shift, and my son was also out. At first, I thought, *what peace!* Lovely. I had a nice long bath to wind down and even dozed in the bath. Afterwards I did feel calmer. After watching a bit of *Comic Relief,* I turned in early, but once I got in bed I don't know why, I couldn't settle. I felt alone again. The house was dead quiet, and my brain was turning over as usual. These days, it seemed to be alone with my thoughts too much. Too much time on my hands, my mum would say. Once I did drift off, I kept waking up because I was too hot. I only remember bits of my dreams, but that was enough to leave me feeling unsettled. My over-active brain was probably the reason I was so tired all the time. I did nothing but think and imagine, and I felt at times like I was going mad. At 7 a.m. I gave up and got out of bed. I was tired, but not too tired. Hubby had just got in from work, and we chatted over coffee before he had to go to sleep. Two more shifts to go yet before he got a break.

On Mother's Day, all my children and grandchildren came over. The house was very noisy, but that had been the usual state of our house when my children were growing up. I laughed; I loved the noise, as it made me feel like nothing had changed over the years. I was so proud of all my children and grandchildren, as nutty as they were. I sat doing nothing, as ordered, as the girls cooked dinner and one of them did my nails. She then suggested we go to a nail bar.

"What, now?" I asked.

"Why not?" she responded, so off we went, leaving everyone behind at the house doing whatever. At the nail bar, we only had to wait five minutes before it was our turn. I had never had my nails done before, and I felt a bit bothered, as I'd seen girls wearing their nails square and didn't like them. So, I told the manicurist no square nails, please, and no French manicure. When he had finished, I was impressed: my nails were in a lovely oval shape and very smooth and I loved the purple nail varnish I had chosen. When get home about an hour later, I show off my nails to everyone. But I wondered, *how on earth can I get things done with longer nails than I'm used to?* After having them on for a bit, I found picking things up rather difficult and I kept fiddling with them. And what a laugh going to the toilet or opening a tin was. I was useless, but it was funny, and I did like them though and planned to keep them and then get them renewed now that I was retired from nursing. Nurses cannot have long, fancy nails because they're a hazard to the health and safety of their patients, and I could never keep my own nails long because they were in water and gel for so long that they always broke or split easily, so I never bothered with them.

When I was on my own, I'd get to looking in the mirror at odd times and still felt like I was Frankenstein's monster, although I never let on about it. *Why did I have to go through all this?* I asked myself. *Does God hate me this much?* But I supposed that everyone on this cancer journey might say the same thing. Sometimes I still get comments like, "You look like you had a fight with a bus," or "They haven't improved you much." The comments do hurt, no one realises even though they are just words" Well I know that, but the hurt is there. Most people close to me told me that my nose improved with each operation, but I never thought so, as I couldn't see any improvement. *Is it me?* I thought. *Or the radiotherapy? Or just bad luck?*

The time dragged as well. People had said to me, "Haven't the years since you got ill gone quickly?" I told them, "Yes, haven't they?" and smiled, I'm sorry but the truth was that the time had dragged so slowly, more slowly than any other period in my life, which was surreal, like just a bad dream. It seemed like my life had been upside down for a long time now. I knew I shouldn't complain, really, as there were so many people worse off than me, and I had seen them at the hospital either while I was working as a nurse or getting treatment as a patient. I felt sad for some patients at the sight of them because they looked so sad and tired. I realised that I'm very lucky to have got this warning, and I am determined to fight all the way, but doing so was hard. Feeling sorry for myself wouldn't help. I'm lucky to be alive I know that, I could at least thank the Lord that I was alive. Besides, I had too much to do before I decide to give up.

Who knows where this illness will lead me. The doctor had told me it would take at least a year to finish the reconstruction and to get my health and vitality back. Until this point, have not cried over my situation. *What's the point?*, I thought. *I have cancer and must deal with it.* I couldn't change the diagnosis, but I could change what I did about it. Looking back, I realised I'd had a full and mainly happy life with ups and downs. I had watched my family grow with pride and love in my heart. I used to be a very strong person in mind and body. *What have I done now?* I asked myself. *I almost threw my life out the window.*

Cancer is one nasty piece of work, but it's not really painful. It's the treatment that's painful and brings you down. I felt drained, so much so that sometimes I couldn't think straight. I had made the decision to retire from work. *Who am I fooling?* I thought. *I can't do this anymore. "Do what"? I ask myself? Carry on the way I am.* The fatigue was painful, and my GP said that I suffered from abscesses and cysts because I was doing too much. She told me that with what I had been through, I couldn't expect for things to stay the same as they were. I knew she was right, but I couldn't accept it. Life went on, and I had to go on as well.

After years of taking care of people, it was an eye opener to be receiving care and to go from nurse to patient, and then from patient to nurse while I was still working. We sometimes get blinkered and blasé in the work we do, I realised. Over the years I'd wept at the loss of some of my patients but also sometimes felt relief that they were no longer in pain.

Do we see that the real suffering is on the inside and not just on the outside? I found that I could go about and appear as happy as my usual self outside, but inside me, in my brain and in my heart, all I felt was hurt and pain. No one else could see that. is this what it's like or is it just me?

Sometimes I thought I had to be a little mad to have my face reconstructed, and maybe it was a foolish idea in the first place. The consultant doing the reconstruction seemed mostly friendly and was at the top of his field, and the construction he had done was remarkable. He had the challenge of starting from nothing, and he had faced it brilliantly. Still, I found him arrogant at times. When we discussed things, I could tell by his face that he didn't listen to me fully, that he wasn't attentive. I also found his secretary impolite and unhelpful. I had seen that most medical or surgery secretaries considered themselves a law unto themselves. They wanted to make decisions when really they didn't have the knowledge or expertise to do so.

I didn't want to retire when I did, but I seemed to have lost the will do anything anymore. I was depressed, and several professionals suggested that I should take antidepressants, but I really didn't want to take more drugs than were necessary.

My GP and the occupational health doctor had been very supportive of my retirement and had contacted the plastic surgeon for information on my diagnosis and treatment and also contacted the consultant about my radiotherapy. The radiotherapy consultant replied and is also in favour of my early retirement, but three months after receiving my application for retirement, the plastics secretary kept coming up with excuses not to respond, such as "the computers are down". I contacted the consultant about this, and in January, he told me he had received the paperwork required for my retirement and would get to it. Well, three months after that, I hadn't heard a peep. This was all so maddening. I felt angry at myself, but I wasn't sure why. And I shouldn't have. After everything that had gone wrong, I still didn't want to give up. Despite this, I felt like I was breaking up inside and no one could feel or hear me. Retiring felt like failing, as my colleagues were short-staffed, and my retirement didn't help.

Still I needed to get paperwork sorted to go through with retirement. I had been told that it just needed to be signed, and that it could take up to a week to get the proper signatures. I couldn't believe it when I heard.

I wanted to shout, "Just sign what's been written and let's get on with it!" I didn't understand why people had to be so unmindful of others? The surgeon's work kept him fully occupied, but I knew from experience that a consultant will do things only when they're good and ready, despite what else is going on, and I know I'm just one more on the pile for this consultant.

Then, after my last interview with the occupational health doctor, the consultant finally signed and faxed my paperwork through that morning. I laughed. How close to the deadline was that I shouldn't have been trying to chase him for the signature, but I hated sitting, waiting, and doing nothing.

I went to see a new occupational health doctor after that, and I was a bit concerned, as I hate having to going over my medical history every time I have to see someone new. I was relieved to find that this doctor was very nice. She went through my retirement papers with me and agreed after reading my medical reports and seeing me that I definitely should be retired. Then I just had to wait for the pension panel to decide if I were entitled to a pension. I didn't understand this process. When doctors and consultants agreed that I should be retired and receive a pension, why should my case then go to a panel of people I had never met so they could decide whether I was entitled? I'm not sure what I would do if they refused. Would I go back to work? Or just stay at home with no money coming in? Life was very stressful already without this worry too. How could people allow anyone with an illness to go through all this? I knew that I'd have to deal with red tape and that the government was reluctant to pay out when someone didn't have a real need and some do take advantage, but why, when I had a legitimate illness, did I have to be in limbo? Do I qualify? I didn't qualify as disabled as such, so what category was I in? Despite the stress, I had to wait for the answer, which would take even longer because of Easter.

When Easter week came around, I bought loads of eggs for my children and grandchildren. I had said that I would only get them for the grandchildren, but, well, I just couldn't help myself. I also got a chocolate orange for my hubby, as they are his favourite. On Good Friday, he complained as he was on shift at work and had not got me an egg. I had already got one from my son, and my nails needed redoing, so I suggested that a manicure could be my Easter gift. My hubby was very happy with that idea, so on Saturday; I went with my niece to the nail bar.

Too many chocolates and being off work was not a good combination for keeping an eye on my weight, but I do love my chocolate. I had to be more careful about what and how much I ate or I would end up as a barrel.

The following week I got a surprise: an answer from the pension board. I was awarded my pension without any more interviews or questions. I supposed that when cancer was involved, they put up few arguments. I rang my boss and told her the news and said that I didn't know when it would be in place or what to do next, so she said she'd ring the head office to find out what the next step was. She was so good to me; that was just one more thing to be thankful for.

April had come, but it was so cold for this time of year, with ice every morning. Where was the sunshine? My niece and her son moved into my house over Easter, so I now had lots of company and with loads of doctor and hospital appointments in April, I'd also have lots to keep me busy.

That first week of April was quite eventful. We were sitting in the living room on Tuesday when the dog, who never makes a peep, suddenly ran to the patio doors. When I looked out, I saw that a lad had jumped over the fence and into my garden. I went out and said, "What do you think you are doing?"

He totally ignored me and went round the side of my house, climbed onto my shed, and went over the neighbour's fence into their garden. When I went back to the patio, a police officer was trying to get over the fence. He was so unfit that I had to laugh. What has happened to the police these days? He eventually got over and met a female officer at the front of the house. The police had lost the man. My neighbour came out the door then, and we really laughed at the unfit police officer.

That Thursday I was off to my GP so she could check out a few lumps on my neck which had been slightly worrying me. At the appointment, she checked my neck and said that what I thought were lumps were nothing. We chatted for a while, and I told her that I felt tearful but didn't know why. She told me that it would not be normal if I didn't feel that way. I then told her about this book, and she laughed and hoped I would write about her favourably. She is a lovely lady and a great doctor.

Following that appointment, I had nothing to do but sit around twiddling my thumbs as I waited for the hospital to give me the date for my next operation and for an "ill-health dismissal meeting" at work, which apparently would include someone from head office, the two ward sisters, and me speaking informally for about ten minutes. I wasn't sure why I was still waiting and dealing with so much red tape if the meeting was so quick.

CHAPTER 9

A couple of weeks later, the meeting still hadn't been arranged. How hard could it be? I felt stressed and impatient with the whole lot, as I couldn't arrange anything in my life until all the operations and the meeting were scheduled. "Dismissal meeting" sounded funny for retirement and not very nice; it sounded more like a meeting about a sacking than getting a pension, and my boss agreed with me and we did have a laugh over the terminology. Even so, I thought I was annoying my boss by constantly asking, "When is it going to be?" I did not mean to nag like a child, so I hoped she wouldn't get to upset with me. She has done so much for me already that I didn't want to rock the boat.

Every day I waited for something, anything in the post from either party, but, still there was nothing. The week had been busy, though. One of my daughter's friends planned on getting married the following year, so we decided to go wedding shopping together. I have not known the friend long and had just met her at parties at my daughter's, but as the week progressed, we found we have a lot in common, and the week turned out to be lovely. I found my daughter's friend very nice and we got on well as we searched the Web for venues. She wanted her dream wedding, of course, and I was determined to help her get it.

We also went shopping for the perfect wedding dress. At one shop, the woman working there turned her back on us. Did we not look rich enough to shop there? What does she know? The man who owned the shop showed us a few of the dresses, but weren't too impressed, so we then went to lunch at my favourite restaurant, Chinese Buffet. Yum! My daughter's friend had never been there before but loved it.

After the lovely lunch, we were off to a very upmarket wedding-gown shop at the other end of the high street. As we entered, one of the ladies greeted us and immediately and chatted with us for a while about what my daughter's friend was looking for, and she made an appointment for my daughter's friend to try on some dresses for the following day. I got home at about 9.30 p.m.; I was tired but had had a good day.

The next morning I collected my daughter's friend and brought her into town. Since her appointment at the dress shop was at midday, we decided to have a bite to eat first, so we went to a cafe for a full late breakfast. The employees at the shop welcomed us warmly, and we sat down to discuss what sort of dress my daughter's friend had in mind. My daughter's friend and I then spent the next few hours enjoying our time as she got into different wedding dresses. The dresses were so beautiful, and my daughter's friend looked amazing in them. She only had to try on three or four to make her decision, and she made the order.

I took my daughter's friend home then, and as we talked about the dresses and the ladies in the shop, she was glowing, and I was very pleased for her. I had taken a lot of pictures on my phone, and when I got home, Hubby downloaded them to the computer so I could email them to my daughter's friend.

The following Saturday, I did the shopping early because my nephew was due to come over that day. In the afternoon, we spent some time gardening, as he had started growing his own sunflowers. He seemed to enjoy making a mess outside, but that's kids for you. Later on, he and his mum went to the park and then came back to help me cook dinner, which he thought was great fun. That evening whilst waiting for dinner, everyone played happily on the Wii till suppertime. After supper, it was a bath and then off to bed for the little lad.

On Saturday morning a week later, I was feeling quite tired, as I had had a busy day on Friday, and the busyness tends to catch up with me the day after. On Friday, I had an outpatient's appointment with the plastic surgeon. Hubby had to take the day off again to take me there, as we had to drive, and I didn't feel confident going in the car alone. The surgeon was pleased with my progress and told me that after maybe two or three more operations before were we would be done. That was great news.

As the surgeon checked my nose, he explained that he had put in a plate and screws to hold the skull bone in place. I hadn't known that and was a bit surprised but wasn't shocked, though, because as a nurse, I could understand the logic behind not telling me before this appointment. He also told me that the plate and pins would stay in to maintain the structure. He then marked on his notes to put me on the waiting list now for my next operation, which would be my sixteenth operation to date. We went home quite contented.

Afterwards, we had to go and visit my dad to celebrate his eighty-first birthday. I gave him his present, and then Hubby and I took him to the Chinese restaurant my daughters and I had booked for the occasion. At the restaurant we met my daughters, their partners, and my two granddaughters. We had a lovely meal. The staff were very attentive clearing plates and serving drinks, and then they produced a cake with candles after the meal and even sang "Happy Birthday to You" with us. Dad smiled and laughed; I think he had a good birthday.

The next morning I got up early after I had not had a good sleep again. I was deadly tired as usual, and I've got used to sleeping three or maybe four hours a night. This made me think about my mum. I never saw her fatigue or pain till the last few days of her life, and then I saw them in her face. *I'm so sorry, Mum,* I thought. *I never realised how much pain and fatigue you felt from working every day and coming home to a full house each night and from helping your neighbours with their illnesses, problems, and housework, running around for everyone else and disregarding how you felt. I was so proud to have you as my mother but never truly realised the impact cancer had on your life. My tears fall for you. I miss you so much. You never gave up; you were stronger than me.* I don't think I truly realised how sad she was after my brother died, although I did know that she never got over her grief—I don't think anyone does—and my heart went out to her, and I tried to help her but didn't know how. I don't know how people carry on, but they do. Everyone says how strong I have been, but you Mum made me understand that strength doesn't make people carry on; they carry on because they have no choice. Dad doesn't mention Mum very much. He seemed to have forgotten most things these days, and even if I started talking about Mum, he changed the subject. I had found this very hard to take in, but I supposed that his memory wasn't so good simply because he was getting older.

Soon after we had the first warm day of the year, and the kids decided that a barbecue would be fun. They all brought food, as was usual lately because there were so many of us that having everyone chip in saved me from having to buy and prepare all the food. All my lovely children and grandchildren attended. My grandson was nearly eight months old now and growing. He was so handsome. My granddaughters were growing fast, too. I love them all so much.

However, even though everyone was here, I did not feel very happy. Oh I go through the emotions and do feel good here and there, but Instead, I felt stressed because my hubby was not feeling well and seemed to be taking it out on me. When he lit the fire, I picked up the poker to stoke it, but he shouted at me as if I was going to do something I shouldn't. Petty, as I knew but I can't seem to shake it off. I know him too well though as that he tended to shout *to* me but not *at* me when he got upset, but I couldn't cheer up after that.

When the food was cooked, I sat and chatted with the family, but I was still very stony, and I knew everyone could tell something was up. A bit later, I smiled at the kids and cuddled with them which always made me feel better till it was time for them to go home.

When everyone had gone, a terrible tiredness came over me. I don't know why so I thought I'd go and have a soak in the bath, as that always relaxes me.

I told Hubby, "If I'm in there a long time, leave me be," as I tended to doze in the hot water.

I rinsed my hair and stepped into the bath, and as I lay there, my brain ticked over as usual about nothing in particular, and the stressed feeling wouldn't go away. I started to feel pain in my chest and realised I needed to get out, it's getting very uncomfortable. I'd had pains like this on and off for about six months but didn't really let on that they were bothering me. Once the pain eased, I sat back down in the bath, and boom, there the pain was again, so I gave up on the bath.

I was just so fed up today and felt that my day had been marred by who knows what. I don't like it I even wrote on my Facebook page that today I felt as if I was losing the will to live. That was just my thoughts running wild as usual, and I knew I would get over it as usual and get on with life.

When I got out of the bath, everyone had gone to bed and the house was quiet. I loved the quiet, and my brain finally settled down. I had heard that there was going to be a meteor shower sometime in the next few nights, so I spent the next two nights gazing at the sky looking for meteors until late. Hubby came downstairs to see if I was okay, and I told him about the meteor shower. He brought out his binoculars and looked with me, but the shower wasn't very visible because the starlight wasn't very strong. Even so, I was very pleased to see three shooting stars, as the sight was unusual. Clouds rolled in at about 2 a.m., and I was getting tired, so I went off to bed.

I got up the morning still feeling very fed up. A violent cramp in the backs of my legs woke me up. I'd experienced night cramps like this for about twenty odd years, and received medication that kept them at bay at times, except when I'm really stressed out, as I had been the previous night.

When I got downstairs, I found my niece lying down on the floor because her back hurt, she said. I'd given her pain relief, but it wasn't working, so I gave her a bit of a massage, which worked instantly. Up she got to get organised. Later, I took her out to lunch, as I thought it would be nice to relax and have some us time. We went to Harvester and were at ease and having fun. Getting out and relaxing helped us to see things so differently, and we were both in a much better frame of mind after the meal, although my niece's poor back was still playing her up.

The days seem to be getting longer as I wait around, I m walking myself around in circles without knowing what to do about her situation or mine. God, life was getting me down. I wished everyone would disappear and leave me alone that day. I had to have everyone else's problems and chores in my lap, because that's me, because I would never turn anyone away, especially family, but this was very hard to bear. For a few days I had had nosebleeds on and off, and I put them down to all the tension and stress around me at the moment. *It's just a nosebleed,* I told myself, but I planned to get them checked out at my oncology appointment later in the week. Who would have thought that after all this time, I would still be worrying about symptoms of cancer? I worry about every change in my body, but after speaking to others in my situation, I learnt that worrying like this was quite normal.

On the day of my appointment with the oncologist, I wasn't too bothered, and I did feel very well. I had to go on my own, as Hubby was on the night shift, but I'm a big girl and was capable of going on my own. When I got to the office, I booked in and wait, and before long, a nurse called me in to be weighed. I knew I'd put on weight because I hadn't been working or exercising, so It was no great shock to me that I had put on half a stone. Really, that wasn't much considering I'd been lazing around for six months, but I planned to join a local gym as soon as my operations were over and I felt well enough to exercise.

About thirty minutes later, I was called in to see the doctor. The oncologist was very friendly and put me at ease to chat, so I told her about what had been happening in the last year since I'd seen her. She then checked me over, and I asked whether the cancer was still in remission, because I my health of late had made me feel a bit nervous. The doctor assured me that I'm doing very well and that I looked well and was still in remission after two years, but she brought up the issue of my smoking. The last time I saw her, I had, in fact, given up, but I as my stress level had risen lately, I couldn't seem to help myself. She wasn't too happy and asked me to try my best to stop again. I told her I would, but I wasn't really in the right frame of mind to quit then, and I felt I had more important things to worry about than whether I smoked. The doctor smiled at me and seemed to understand. I thanked her and felt quite good as I drove home.

The next morning I finally received a letter with details of the "dismissal meeting", my final work interview. I decided to have Hubby come with me for support. The letter made it sound more formal than I had been told it would be, as it gave the impression that there were problems because the wording was scary as it indicated that I might need a union rep with me. I couldn't fathom why I would need one there. If it's as informal as I was lead to believe, so I rang my boss to confirm the date and tell her that Hubby would attend with me but that I didn't feel any need for the union rep to be there. She agreed with me, which put my over-active mind at ease. I needed to stop over-reacting at everything thing but there is really so much going on around me that I just let my feelings get the better of me.

But as the week progressed, the drama continued. My daughter and her family were going away for the weekend, so I agreed to take them to the airport at 4 a.m. I didn't mind, as my son in law takes Hubby and me to the airport when we go away. Off I went to fill the car with fuel, humming a tune, when Hubby passed me going the other way. "What the—?" I asked myself. When I got home, he told me he had been sent home from work, as he had not been sleeping because he was itchy all over. He had been complaining for a few days that the itchiness had been driving him nuts, but I had put it down to eczema, which he had had on and off as long as I'd known him. I told him then to get to the doctor's. He doesn't like going seeing the doctor, but I told him that if you're going to be off sick from work, then to the doctor's you go.

When he came back from his appointment the following day, he told me that it wasn't eczema but that the doctor wasn't sure what it was and needed to have a blood test to find out. The doctor gave him antihistamines to alleviate the itching, so he had to stay off work until after the results of the blood test came back, as he couldn't work with machinery whilst on the antihistamines. This gave me a slight bit of worry, as he had been disgustingly healthy for all of our married life, but then I realised that since the start of my journey, he'd been sick more frequently. I think that the stress caused by my condition had made him unwell. I couldn't be sure of this until after the test results were in, but I did see a pattern: each time something happened to me, he became sick. On a brighter note, I realised he'd be able to do the airport run in my place, and I laughed to myself. Of course he agreed as I knew he would, so I wouldn't have to get up in the night. What a star he was.

Hubby and I have had a nice week after that spending time doing the gardening and going out to dinner a few times on our own, which made a nice change. My daughter had asked us to look after her family's hamster while they were away, who was getting old and didn't seem right this week, and when we went to feed him on Saturday, we found that he had died in the night. Poor little thing. I put him back in his little house, and we buried him in my daughter's garden. I had to tell her, so I rang her in Ireland.

"I'm so sorry to call you on holiday, but I think you needed to know," I said, and I delivered the news.

"Okay. Thanks, Mum," she said, crying, and that was it.

That evening at about eleven, my neighbour and friend came over crying. Her little dog had passed away. Oh, Lord, two deaths in one day. My neighbour's pet had been unwell and back and forth to the vet for the past few weeks, so she had seen it in the cards. I gave her a big hug and then went to her house to collect all the dog's belongings and give them to my hubby to take to our house, as she was too upset to do this, and I thought it best to remove all the dog's things now rather than later. My neighbour and I then discussed what she should do with her pet. She decided that she didn't want to wait all weekend for the vet's to open, so I helped her to bury the dog in the garden. Poor little mite. At least she had gone peacefully instead of having to be put to sleep.

The next morning I took my neighbour out to the local garden centre, where I had seen a little stone figure that looked just like her dog. She was very pleased with it, so she bought it to mark the dogs grave. The figure looked so nice there, and my neighbour seemed settled, although it would take her a long time to work through her grief, as she loved her dog very much. I said that it was sad that our pets didn't live as long as we would like, and she agreed.

A few days later, the day for my last interview at work had finally come. I was a bit nervous. I chatted to my hubby and I had decided to go on my own because I had chosen to volunteer on the ward till the meeting, and the ward sister was very happy with the idea. Hubby dropped me off around 10.30, and one of the sisters made us coffee and sat and chatted with me a while. She was concerned about how I was feeling, but

I felt very well that day, and I told her it made me feel a bit of a fraud going into my final meeting.

"I think the warm weather and early summer sunshine have helped, too," I said, "and I' have spent the last few days out gardening."

We spent the rest of the morning going around the ward making sure there was no clutter, checking that everything was clean and in working order, and then it was lunch time. The morning had flown by. I had brought a lunch so I could settle with the girls in the sitting room to eat. It was lovely to see them all, and we chatted the whole time about nothing in particular. After lunch, Sister asked if I was okay, as she said she did not want to tire me out, and I assured her I felt good. I then went off to the treatment room to make sure the shelves were tidy, and when I had finished, I was getting a bit weary, so I went back to Sister's office and chatted with her over coffee She thanked me for my help, and I replied that it was my pleasure. I have enjoyed this time on the ward, as it made me feel like I am still useful, but I knew I couldn't keep it up all day. Then the time came for Sister and I to attend the meeting with the managers. The girls hugged me and wished me luck.

When Sister and I went into the meeting room, the three managers were already there. Sister introduced them to me, and they offered me a seat. The managers then read the relevant papers and asked me a few questions. Throughout, they were very kind, and I did not feel stressed or pressured. They asked me how I felt about retiring, and I told them that I felt very sad, as I loved being a nurse, but that I also realised that I needed to be realistic, as I had tried several times to return to work but found that I was too tired to do so anymore. I needed to take retirement to recoup as much strength as I could to feel that I was truly living and not just surviving.

The managers then went through the doctors' reports and then told me that I had met all the criteria to take ill-health retirement, so there were no issues. Then the meeting was finished, and I thanked the managers for their time and made sure to say that the staff on my ward were the best people anyone could work with and to tell Sister from my heart that it had been a pleasure and honour to work for her. She told me to go back to the ward while she and the managers finished the paperwork.

The girls were all waiting for me on the ward to hear the outcome, and stupidly, I just burst into tears. One of the sisters hugged me, and the other girls did too, they were all very kind. After I'd settled down, the sister made me coffee, and we chatted. My colleagues were such lovely people. Luckily, I think I have been given approval to do volunteer work here, so I would see them regularly.

Sister then arrived back on the ward with one of the managers and asked me if I was all right.

I laughed and said, "Yes, I'm fine. I've just had a good cry."

Sister smiled at me as we went into her office, where I signed the last of the paperwork terminating my employment with the NHS. Whilst we were finishing up, all the staff came in as a group and gave me the most beautiful bouquet of flowers and a box of chocolates. I was a bit choked up, but I held my composure and thanked them very much. Everyone hugged me again and suggested that we arrange a retirement meal.

Hubby picked me up about twenty minutes later, and I told him about the outcome of the meeting on the way home. He asked if I was okay, and I told him I was but very sad but would be okay. He said he understood how I felt about retirement.

That evening, another sister from the ward rang me to ask how I had got on, as hadn't been there that day. I told her everything. She is a lovely person and was very understanding. She was the one who one day as we were sitting in our staff room had said to me, "You know, you've had an eventful three years. You should write a book about it." We laughed about the idea at the time—I wasn't a writer—and I didn't think about it again till recently. She was due to retire herself in three months and was already feeling the shock of getting to retirement age, so she knew how I felt. I told her that she had such a fantastically busy life outside the hospital that I was sure her days would be full when she stopped working. She commented that work had interfered with her social life, and we laughed. We chatted some more, and then I told her I would see her soon on the ward.

I finally realised, as the sister had told me on the phone, that retirement wasn't an end but a beginning. I could now concentrate on my children, grandchildren, and friends. I'd be able to join the gym when all my operations were finished. And maybe, in a year's time, I could look into joining a volunteer group to help other cancer patients who feel as I had felt; I think that this experience has given me greater insight into how cancer treats people and how it impacts their lives. I thought that as a nurse, that I was fully open to how others felt, but my eyes weren't really open until the day I was diagnosed with cancer.

On a bank holiday weekend shortly after, everyone I cared about was off work at the same time, which was unbelievably rare. My auntie rang Friday, and I said, "Come to dinner on Sunday. All the kids and grandkids are going to be here." She loved the idea, as she adores seeing everyone and had been in their lives as long as she had been in mine. My uncle is also my son's godfather, and the two of them are great fun to be around.

As I bought the food for the dinner party, I thought I had to be mad to have twelve people for dinner. Oh well. Our family had grown so much over the years that I was getting used to big get-togethers.

My niece had worried me a bit, although she was starting to sort her life out, but she told me that if I wanted, she could stay at my daughter's house during the dinner.

"What?" I said. "Certainly not. You will be here with the rest of the family,"

She said she felt that she was in the way, but I told her she was a dope for feeling like that, and we loved her very much regardless of what she did in life. She seemed okay then, and I was glad I had a little chat with her as it always helps to clear the air.

Ten minutes later I had a run-in with my son, which seems to happen a lot with him. When he's tired, he gets fed up with the world and freely admits his depressive moods, but we clash often, and he makes little comments that can be very rude to me, not just in private either even when we have guests he aims at me,. He had been doing this for a couple of years, and I didn't know why I put up with it. My daughters often got angry at me about him. "Why is he still living at home?" they'd say. "He is old enough to grow up and get a life." But he wouldn't. He wouldn't use his clever brain as he should have, although he was doing well in his university studies. He didn't seem to realise how his inappropriate behaviour and attitude affected others and when I would confront him about it, he went up to his room saying that we obviously didn't want him around. Sometimes I worried about his mental stability, as I think he still lived at home because he wasn't stable enough to live on his own. But I am very proud of his achievements But life goes on, and I always let him go off to his room to stew, realising that the very next day he would appear downstairs as if nothing had happened and give me a cheerful, "Morning, Mummy," It goes to show that his heart was mostly in the right place. I give up.

On Saturday night, I couldn't sleep, as Hubby was tossing all over in the bed, so at 6 a.m. I gave up and got up after only three hours' sleep. I was very tired, but I tried to ignore the feeling, as I had a lot to do that day. I got myself a coffee, and by 7 a.m., the meat for the dinner party was in the oven, as I like meat to cook slowly but well and leave it in the oven for hours. Then I sat quietly in the kitchen peeling what seemed like hundreds of potatoes, but finally dinner was prepared. The peace was lovely, but still I was so very tired. *Pick yourself up!* I ordered myself as my son and hubby got up to help me tidy the place a bit.

Everyone had arrived by midday, and with dinner planned for about 3 p.m., we had a chance to chat and catch up with each other. The house got a bit noisy, but I love my noisy family very much. Dinner went off well, and everyone had plenty to eat, including a massive chocolate cake that my aunt had brought.

Later in the afternoon when everyone was getting ready to leave, my granddaughter asked for some sunflowers to take home. I planted them knowing that she'd want them, so we went out to the garden with my little trowel. As I bent down, my nose just poured with blood. Bless her, my granddaughter ran indoors and came out with lots of tissues for me. I had cleaned myself up and held the tissues to my nose for a few minutes, wondering where on earth the nosebleed had come from. The bleeding stopped after a few minutes, and I finally dug up the flowers for my granddaughter and went back in the house. I then went into the bathroom, and there it went again, the blood was pouring down again. My shirt was covered, my husband came to sit with me as I just sat there holding a towel to my face.

"Maybe your blood pressure's up a bit," he said. It had been a tiring and busy day, so I agreed.

Finally, after long a while, the bleeding stopped again. I told Hubby I would keep an eye on my nosebleeds. As the last time I had had such a bad a nosebleed, I was diagnosed with cancer. *Has the cancer come back? I wondered. Don't be silly. It's just a nosebleed*, but I wasn't sure anymore.

Everyone had gone home by then, but we arranged to meet up at my daughter's house the next day for a barbecue. I said I would attend depending on how I felt, but for now all I wanted to do was rest. Hubby told me to go to bed, but it was only 8 p.m., and I knew I'd be up in the night if I went to bed then, so I said not yet.

We then sat down to watch a film, and I think I lasted thirty minutes before I dropped off to sleep, but I didn't go to bed until about 10.30.

I had a restless night and woke up a few times, and by 6 a.m., I was ready to get up. At least I had had a bit of sleep. I was the only one up at that hour, so I made myself a coffee and sat in the quiet.

My nose seemed okay and hadn't bled since the episodes the day before, but I felt a bit of pressure in the top of my nose. I didn't blow my nose for fear that something might happen again but it didn't bother me too much, so I decided nothing sinister was going on.

As bank holiday Monday wore on, my nose felt really blocked, and I can feel the pressure in my forehead. I chose to ignore it again and go to the barbecue.

Everyone was there including some my daughters' old school friends; the weather was lovely out the sun is out. All the guests seemed happy and relaxed. At about 6.30 p.m., I told Hubby that we need to go home to give the poor dog supper and a run, and he agreed, so we said our goodbyes and went home. That night we watched a film, but I dropped off in the middle as usual and went to bed.

In the morning my nose felt blown up and tight, as I had avoided cleaning it out, something I needed to do regularly, as I cannot blow my nose as I had done and didn't produce mucus since losing my septum. I cleaned my nasal passages with a product called St Mark's Electrolyte Mix, a mixture of salt, sugar, bicarbonate of soda, and warm water, which I squirted up my nose every day with a bottle called a doucher before blowing it out. This solution was usually used orally for rehydration for those with short bowel syndrome, but the staff at the head and neck cancer unit had recommended it for my case, and it did the job well. Although I'd had to do the cleaning for the past 2 years, I still hated it, as it gives me a lot of pain in the front of my head, but I have no choice but to do it and would have to do it for the rest of my life. I supposed this was a small price to pay to be free from cancer.

On Tuesday morning my nose was definitely blocked, I guessed because of the nosebleed, and the blockage had worsened to the point that I had to breathe mostly through my mouth. Still I was loath to clean it out, as the headache it would give me seemed worse than the blockage. A few hours later, I finally cleaned out my. I had no great mishaps, and my nose was clean and clear, and I could breathe again. The cleaning wasn't as bad as I thought it would be.

On a lighter note, my niece got a call that morning about a potential job. This was great news for her, and I hoped it meant she could retain custody of her son. We just had to hope and wait. I was sad for her that she still had to go through custody battles, but I hoped it would all be over soon and she could be happy again.

Her situation had given me headaches, as it pushed my stress levels high, and that day, my head was banging away. I just wanted to sit quietly all the time. I wondered whether it was normal for people who'd had surgery to their heads to feel such pain or whether I was just a weakling.

I keep wondering whether all this stress would bring back the cancer. I was supposed to be resting, but that wasn't happening. I was still waiting to hear about my next operation, but hadn't heard from the hospital, leaving my mind to do me in. What was the matter with them? All I did day after day was sit around playing games on the Web, watching television, and losing days of my, although I didn't have any inclination to get up and go. I said to myself that I wanted to do things but just don't seem to be able to get up and do them. *Why am I am wasting my life?* I wondered. After losing my work and people I loved, I'd got to a stage where I didn't feel alive. Did other people who'd gone through the same things feel the same? I hoped not all because this was not a nice feeling. My doctor had said this lethargy was to be expected because of the journey I'd been on in the last several years, and that sounded like a good excuse, but was it the truth? Perhaps I just needed a push to do things, be more active. I go out shopping and do the housework because I have to, but that's it. As a rule I used to rush and run everywhere, and I loved to do things and go places, to the point where Hubby used to say we needed an appointment to see each other, which I have to say was very true and I thought life was great then.

Hubby and I booked a week's holiday for the beginning of June. The surgeons still had not given me a date for my next surgery, so I decided, stuff it, let's go. For once, people could wait for me because I'm fed up with sitting around and waiting for things to happen.

I rang the surgeon's secretary to give her the dates of the holiday, and blast that woman! She was quite rude, her tone was very cold, and she hardly gave me a chance to say anything.

When I rang, I said, "Good morning. I am waiting for further surgery."

She stopped me there and said, "We don't have a date for you yet. Why are you ringing? We will let you know when a date is fixed."

"Excuse me," I said, "but that is not why I'm calling. I'm just ringing to let you know I will not be around on these dates," and I gave her the dates.

"Yes, well, I will make a note of that." She replied and rang off.

Dealing with her and the whole surgical team had left me feeling slightly bitter. Well, that's it, I decided. I won't ring again. I'd have been willing to bet that letter would then arrive with a date for surgery smack bang in the middle of my holiday, but I wouldn't changing my dates for anyone. I was trying to sort out other things in my life then, too, and it was not going too well. Everyone, including some members of my family, seemed uncooperative. This left me feeling quite bratty.

CHAPTER 10

The week rolled away, and I was quite busy doing the things that needed doing for my family, such as shopping, and by the end of the week, I was so tired. Two of my girls wanted to do a car boot sale, so I said, why not?, but then I realised I had to have been mad. On Sunday morning I was up at 5.45 a.m. so I could pick up one daughter at her house by 6, but I needed to text her first to remind her to make a flask of coffee because my coffee pot broke. We got to the sale at about 6.30, and it was chilly but not too bad as the sun came up. After about an hour my elder daughter arrived, and we all pitched in and had a laugh. I really enjoyed the sale, as it was so very relaxing to sit all morning doing nothing but chatting. The girls were so funny—after they sold things, they immediately went off to buy things, and it looked like we'd be bringing home as much as we had brought to sell. A lady near us put some music on, and we all sang to "Running Bear", a great song that cheered us all up so well. Later in the morning my daughter left her daughters with me and went off to wander with her hubby. I loved chatting with the girl's mainly about silly things and my younger granddaughter is very cuddlesome this morning, I love it. When we got home that evening, ten people had come over for dinner, so I cooked for the lot. I loved having them, but the cooking and entertaining was hard work, so I was glad when they went home. After a while, I sat in my chair and went straight off to sleep. It was a good day—I felt no pain, and no odd thoughts went around in my head I'm glad to say.

I thought I would have a good night after such a good day but the following morning I woke up feeling like death. When I looked in the mirror in the bathroom, I looked so old and didn't see myself anymore. The lump of skin the surgeon had left on the side of my nose looked like a lump of spare meat. Oh, God, I hate it! I resented the cancer for making me look like this. I ached all over and I felt angry and frustrated all day that this illness had restricted what I was able to do and kept me from doing what I wanted to do. My doctor had told me these feelings were a common reaction to cancer and its treatment and that I shouldn't feel guilty about having such thoughts or feelings but I couldn't help it. Is it like this for everyone? I wondered whether I had thought about how cancer patients felt before this and whether I had missed something in the care I delivered while I was working. I truly hoped that never happened, as I was mortified at the possibility.

Hubby made me a drink and asked if I was okay, and I told him I didn't feel great today. I'm sure everyone must feel this way sometimes, but I didn't like it feeling so different. Later on in the day, I felt much better. It's funny how certain things can just turn your mood around.

That morning I answered a phone call, to well I don't know who and the person on the other end kept saying, "Hello, sir. Hello, sir," and then something about life insurance.

I got angry and shouted, "I don't want life insurance, I can't understand half of what you are saying, and I'm not a sir! Goodbye!" and I slammed the phone down.

My husband, who was sitting behind me suddenly, hooted with laughter, and I had to join in. How many hundreds of people got a call like this? After the laughter had died down, I felt so much better and was ready to take on the day. It's true when they say laughter really is the best medicine. Bring on the rest of the day.

Hubby had finally gone back to work that day after having about a month off. *Peace,* I thought, but then, blimey, two hours later he was back home. "What now? Did they sack you?" I asked.

He told me that after about an hour at work, he had started itching again, so the boss had sent him home. It was back to the doctor's for more blood tests then. Hubby brought his work clothes home to wash them here rather than at work, as the doctor suspected my hubby could possibly have an allergy to the detergent used on the safety clothing. So I have washed the lot.

In the morning Hubby got himself ready, and then we had a bit of a stress as I tried to explain where the blood testing office was at the hospital. He didn't get it.

"For goodness sake!" I said. "It's not rocket science. Do you want me to come with you?"

"No, I will find it," he responded.

Oh, Lord, give me strength to deal with this man who knows everything, I thought. *Maybe I should move out.* Life at home seemed to be getting harder to cope with. On top of Hubby's problem, we have had to ask our niece to move out that week. I love her very much, but I was stuck because I couldn't have my granddaughters sleep over while she was here, and after not having them here for more than a month, I did miss them so. This was a hard decision, but I know my niece understood that having an extra adult living here with me was very tiring and, more important, that she needed to go and get her life back together.

My niece moved out that weekend, but Hubby and I stored most of her things in the spare room, as she wasn't able to take much more than the necessities with her until her flat was ready. Life at home felt almost normal again, but I was a bit worried though because she hadn't telephoned to say she was all right, and I texted her and rang her mobile several times without success. I didn't know what she was doing with herself.

Two days later, my daughter rang, and I agreed to have the granddaughters after school. I loved collecting the little one from primary school, as she always threw herself at me and gave me the biggest hugs. When my older granddaughter came in, however, she was not in a very good frame of mind, I asked her to get out of uniform before dinner, but she was still in it when I served dinner. I kept quiet about it. After supper I asked her to do her homework, as she had an assignment due the next day, and she became really stroppy. She couldn't understand what she needed to do in some places, so she refused to do the assignment. When I asked if she wanted some help, she almost bit my head off. I was quite annoyed with her, I don't usually get very angry with any of them but she was now going on thirteen, a terrible age. I knew her attitude was mainly caused by hormones, but that didn't change the fact that she was rude.

When I got home from the younger girl's school run the next day, I felt so deadly tired, so I rang my daughter and told her I wouldn't collect the girls on Friday because I couldn't deal with the older girl's moods. I felt like a coward. I had dealt with my own kids' hormones while they were growing up, so why did I feel differently about my granddaughter? I would have liked to think I was just older now, but I wondered whether it was really because my self-confidence was still at a low. Who knows, but anyway the next morning I received a text from my granddaughter with a lovely apology, and can forgive her for everything as we do and promised her and her sister that I would be there to collect them at the end of the week. I didn't like to tell my granddaughter off, but she needed to understand that she had to understand right from wrong and deal with her rage in a more productive way.

My nursing registration, a program that allows qualified nurses to practice and, as required by law, must be renewed yearly with a fee and proof of approximately thirty hours of continuing education, was due by the end of the month, the paperwork from the nursing authority I received every year reminded me. With a heavy feeling inside I have telephoned the registry to inform them that I would not be renewing my registration and explained the reasons. The person I spoke to was very kind and told me that if I wished to renew in the next few years, I wouldn't have much of a problem doing so, as procedures were in place for to do so. The doctors had informed me that it wasn't very likely that I could return to work, but it cheered me a little to know that ending my registration wasn't completely the end of my career. But I still felt lost and alone sometimes because of it, I know I'm not alone but it doesn't change the way all this has made me feel. I snapped myself out of it, as it was no use moaning over something I couldn't change. Life has a funny way of dealing with us as we go on, and ups and downs continue no matter what, so figured I might as well enjoy my retirement while it lasted.

Another bank holiday weekend came up again shortly after, and the whole family got together. My eldest came over with the baby for the day, and we played with him and had a lovely chat. I decided I wanted to have the baby stay here overnight sometime soon, but I needed to get a cot first, as he had outgrown his carrycot. I scoured the Web to find one and ended up buying a baby swing for the garden.

Hubby laughed. "I thought you were looking for a cot," he said.

"I was, but I found this swing, so I bought it."

My youngest daughter arrived after that with her partner, my niece, and my niece's son. My daughter brought me a birthday present even though my birthday wasn't for another week, but as she would be on holiday then. She insisted I open it right away so she could see that I liked it. I opened the package to find a lovely sunhat and an outfit to go with it.

"How lovely! Thank you," I said. "These are very pretty." They were just right for my holiday in Tenerife two weeks later. I felt very contented and very lucky to have such a family.

A fair was on for the bank holiday in a local park it is a huge park, with miles of space along the canal with children's pools, a play space for the little ones, and a little train for the children. It is a truly beautiful park, and Hubby and I took our kids there to play and have picnics when they were small. I was pleased that they'd carried on the tradition with their own children. Everyone at our house arranged to meet up with my other daughter, her hubby, and their girls an hour later.

We had got separated on the way, and my youngest girl, who is so funny, rang me to ask where I was, and I described our location and then asked where she was, and she said, "We are by a tree."

Hubby and I laughed so much, and when I caught my breath, I said, "Which tree is that, honey?"

My daughter went quiet for a minute and then suddenly burst out laughing. She hadn't realised that we wouldn't be able to find her by "a tree" out of the many thousands of trees are in the park!

Finally we got our locations sorted and met in the fairground and wandered around it for a while just watching. My daughters all went on the fast, high rides. I loved these when I was younger but couldn't get enthusiastic about them anymore. In fact, I felt ill just watching them going round, so I volunteered to hold the handbags and watch the grandchildren.

Hubby then said, "You always loved the Waltzer. Let's go on it."

"Why not?" I said, so when the girls got back, I handed everything over to them, and off Hubby and I went, my youngest granddaughter, wanted to go on it with me so I took her too. The Waltzer spun around and around very fast, and I really enjoyed it, and although my granddaughter screamed, she loved it too. The ride seemed to go on longer than I remember, but it was fun the whole time. When it finally stopped and we got off, I felt a bit heady but not too bad. I was pleased that I could still go on this one, but there was still no way I was going on the other rides.

When everyone was getting ready to go a bit later, I bought a bag of candy floss, which I love. It's so sticky and a bit naughty, but who cares? Then most of the kids left, and Hubby and I went with my daughter, son-in-law, and granddaughters down the hill to the kids' area. It was about 3.30 p.m. by then and getting hot, so the kids wanted to paddle in the pool. I told them to go for it, and they took me at my word and went in fully clothed!

Whilst the girls played, we adults sat with coffees and watched them. The monkeys sat in the pool, fully clothed under the waterfall and got drenched. I loved it and laughed. My daughter groaned, but I reminded her that when I was younger, even I rushed into the water in my clothes whilst on holiday with my parents. She laughed then, so all was good.

When the girls finally came out, they had a drink and then rolled around on the grass together and laughed. It was lovely to see how well they got on.

My head was getting very hot by this point, as I had not brought a hat, as usual, so we all decided to go back to my daughter's house and finish the day with pizza. We had had a lovely day, but by about 8.30 p.m., I suddenly felt really tired. I told Hubby I needed to go home, and he agreed. Once at home, I went straight to bed. The day had totally worn me out.

I woke up at 1 a.m. feeling hot and sweaty, so I went downstairs for a coffee and then went back to bed. I tossed and turned until I got up at 6 a.m. I had thought I would get a good night's sleep after the day out, but no. Oh well another day.

That day I wanted to go out, but it was raining as had been usual. Although it was the end of May, the April showers hadn't stopped. I searched the Web for a place where I could go with family without getting wet, and then I rang my son-in-law, and we took the girls out for most of the day, just the four of us, as my daughter was at work. We went bowling and had a lot of fun. How can I be beaten by a seven-year-old, but she did have the barriers up in her lane, and she high-fived us after each turn. We had really worked up an appetite by the end of our games, so we went to Harvester for dinner. When I returned home, I just flopped. I was quite tired but not overly worn out.

The next day was my birthday—I was fifty-five years old and already out of work. It had just gone midnight when Hubby came into the room and presented me with a mini apple pie.

"Happy birthday, darling," he said. "I couldn't find a candle."

I just laughed; he could be such a nutter at times. I then asked, "Am I a pensioner now, or am I just retired?"

He laughed and said, "You are not a pensioner, love. You're just taking time off."

"Okay," I said. "Just making sure." Then we went to bed. I've had a busy day but a good one.

In the morning I woke to about thirty Facebook messages wishing me a happy birthday, and all my children rang me, so I had a nice start to the day. My aunt and uncle then came over to take me out to lunch as a birthday treat. My aunt picked a carvery just down the road, so I told her I would drive, as that was easier than giving directions. The restaurant was very nice there, and we chatted whilst we ate. My uncle was a barrel of laughs. I loved being with them.

Two of my girls had told me that they would take me out for a birthday dinner the next day because they had had to work during my actual birthday, but I had already been out for three birthday dinners. *Oh, Lord, I thought. I'm going to get fat.* Eating out was all I seemed to be doing lately, but I couldn't complain. That day, my daughters told me, "Leave your purse at home. You are not paying for anything. We'll pick you up later."

When dinnertime came, two of my daughters, their partners, and all three of my grandchildren were there, a really lovely little party, went to a Greek restaurant, one of my favourites. The staff provided excellent service as usual, and the food was divine—I was eating for England. At the end of the meal, the manager brought out a birthday cake and sang "Happy Birthday to You" with my family. "Love the cake" I told my daughter, she had sprayed the cake gold, which was lovely. "I hope it's not enamel paint," I joked. I ended up taking the whole cake home; I couldn't have touched any more food if I had tried.

After all the food I've eaten this week, I decided that was it—I was officially on a diet. So, in the few days following the dinner at the Greek restaurant, I had been living on cereal and salads, and I planned to keep eating like this until I felt comfortable, because bloating did not feel good.

I was so lucky to have such caring and loving children. Bringing them up was certainly a feat, and I'm so proud of how they've matured and what they've achieved. Sometimes I get choked up—happily, mind you—just looking at them all. We realise we all have our own paths to lead and don't live in each other's pockets, although we are a close family, and I wouldn't have it any other way.

On Tuesday, Hubby finished his last night shift before our holiday to Tenerife on Friday. We hadn't even started packing, as it was my husband's habit to leave everything possible to the last minute. This was infuriating at times because when I would start to pack, he'd say, "Leave it. I'm going to do it," as he thought he packed cases better than I did, so I would leave them, as I couldn't be bothered to argue. We did finally finish packing on Thursday afternoon. On Friday, our son-in-law took us to the airport at 4.30 a.m. for the flight at 7. I don't seem to be as excited about the trip as usual and was very tired, and I didn't know why. I tried to shrug the feeling off, and I thought I'd be fine in a bit, but I wasn't sure.

"Something bugging you?" my hubby asked.

"I don't know," I replied. "Hopefully we'll have a good week."

I had been expecting a restful week, but Hubby wanted to hire a car to go up the mountain. He also wants to go to one of the lovely parks to see a bird show. I didn't mind doing a few things, so I agreed.

On the first few days of the holiday, we did lots of exploring and then sat in the hotel garden watching the entertainment every evening. The entertainers were quite talented, and I enjoyed the shows, but the weather was cold in the evenings. This was unusual, and I felt so uncomfortable, but as I looked around no one else seemed all that bothered about the temperature, so I told myself to ignore it, but it wreaked havoc on my sleep. I woke every two hours, and when I did drift off, my dreams were jumbled and loud, leaving me feel worse each morning.

One evening we met a nice couple in the hotel garden and found we had the same love of dogs. We chatted most of the evening till bedtime and met them again over the next few days for a chat and a laugh about nothing in particular. I tried to enjoy the days, but I couldn't seem to get with it, and I seem to be getting very sunburnt even though I was careful to stay out of the full sun each day and to wear my hat at all times.

On Wednesday we went out on a ship to see the dolphins and whales, and seeing them in their home out in the sea was something I loved. The weather was nice, but I stayed at the back of the boat in the shade.

On Thursday, the last full day of our holiday, when I woke up and tried to stand, the room was spinning, and I need to lie down again and shut my eyes. I slept for another hour, and when I got up again, the spinning returned. On the way to the toilet I felt like I was walking sideways swaying as if I were drunk. I had to go back to bed again. A bit later, Hubby suggested I go to breakfast with him, and I agreed. He had to help me on the way, and I managed to have something to eat, but I still felt poorly. I told him I couldn't go anywhere and asked him to take me back to the room, and I needed to lie down again and slept till about lunchtime. Hubby then suggested a short walk, so I went. We took it slowly, as I still didn't feel well at all. We had lunch at a local cafe and then went back to the hotel. We wandered into the garden area and had a cold drink, and suddenly I felt dizzy again. He took me back up to the room, and I slept till 4 p.m. Hubby was reading when I woke up. He was very good to me and didn't moan even though we spent most of the day in the room. He told me he was worried about me and that it was fine with him if I rested. I felt a bit better by evening, and I thought about what had caused my illness. I couldn't believe it—for the first time in Tenerife, I think I managed to get sunstroke. Just my luck. The last full day of our holiday and I'm ill. We flew home the next day, and I felt a lot better, and I was looking forward to my own bed.

The following week, Hubby went to work, and the house was quiet in the morning, so I checked the post. Still no word from the hospital. Blast them! Why were they still doing nothing? I thought they might have intended to really stretch out the rest of my operations. The surgeon had never left me without contact this long between appointments or operations. Well, it was no use moaning, as others were worse off than me, but I still can't help feeling a bit annoyed.

Later that day, I asked all my children to come on holiday to Tenerife in the next year with my hubby, their kids, and me. This would be a riot and much better than sitting around moaning about things I couldn't do anything about or change.

I was still worried about my health, as I felt hot and my whole back, my neck, and my head ached. I think I have put it down to the stress and strain of having to wait around to find out what to do next. I also felt nauseated, and the mild dizziness I had thought was sunstroke had returned. One night after we had returned home, my hubby was snoring so loudly that I put earplugs in, and suddenly the room was spinning, and I had to take the earplugs out. I didn't get much sleep again that night. The next day I was so deadly tired that I was in pain. Hubby wouldn't leave me alone, constantly asking if I was all right, suggesting various remedies and saying he knew how I felt. This was aggravating—no one but me could have known how I felt—and I kept telling him so, but he thought he knew best. Again. But sometimes I had to laugh at the irony of his causing me further stress by trying to be supportive. I was ready to scream, but I didn't let on that day he drove me nuts, as his intentions were good. I could be a little horrid. Because I know he loves me and worries about me,

He told me when we were on holiday that he had been so scared when I was diagnosed with cancer. I could understand; the thought of losing someone so close would be frightening for anyone, as I knew from the experience of losing loved ones as have a lot of people. We go through the initial fear, the pain and the loss. But his feelings had caused some tenseness in our relationship because he didn't have anyone else at home to support him emotionally. The stress of dealing with my illness had affected his physical health; too as in he never used to go to the doctors so I know he is run down with the strain it has caused. My journey had taught me that if I didn't seek out mental and physical support, I wouldn't receive it, and my husband didn't know how to seek support in this way.

I'd wondered whether my cancer was serious enough to warrant outside help, and I'd believed that I was supposed to simply go on by myself, but not having the support I needed made me feel lost and alone for most of the time but we go on because that's what we believe we are supposed to do in our minds. Apart from having to cope with the physical and medical challenges of cancer, I also had to face worry and other feelings and concerns are unique to someone with this disease, and I'd learnt that attending to my emotional health was often as important to my life as attending to my physical health. A support group could have helped me feel less isolated and distressed and could have improved my quality of life. In addition, such support groups often provide patients with the most current information regarding available treatments. Anyone suffering from an uncommon form of cancer such as mine should consider joining a specialised online community to gain such support and additional information that might not be available anywhere else.

CHAPTER 11

A cancer diagnosis is a life-altering event. I experienced anxiety at the time of diagnosis, at the onset of the treatment, and when moving from active treatment to follow-up care, and even though my cancer is in remission, I still experience symptoms of depression. It isn't uncommon. Even though I was a nurse, I still found that my family and I were unprepared for the emotional burdens of this experience, and I know my experience as a nurse-turned-patient isn't unique. Nurses are only human, after all. However, since my diagnosis, I believe I've adapted fairly well to the challenges that have arisen and have found ways to deal with the unpredictability and vulnerability associated with this illness.

Now when I look in the mirror, I see someone completely different from the person I was before my diagnosis. I don't see me anymore, and I don't like how that makes me feel. I don't particularly like the way I look from the nose down. I look rather bigger than I did before, although I'm not surprised by my weight, as apart from walking the dog and walking around on holiday, I haven't done any exercise. Feeling lethargic most days doesn't help, It's like I'm caught in a vicious circle: I'm tired because I'm not doing much, but I'm also too tired to actually do anything about it.

Since my diagnosis, I have had very mixed feelings about the attitudes of the many health professionals I've seen. I have felt let down that my previous GP misdiagnosed my cancer, seeing only the symptoms of flu and colds. He obviously thought here we go another nose problem. Why didn't he look more closely or even write down more information in my records? It saddens me that some doctors don't listen to patients at times when we patients know our own bodies best. When I see stories in the news telling of a doctor catching cancer in the early stages, I know that this isn't a universal experience for those with cancer, as others like me slip through the net.

I'm lucky I'm still alive, but I feel the loneliness, I know it's mostly my own fault. The way my face looks has caused me to shy away from being in public. When I am out, I always seemed to think that people had nothing better to do than stare at me or talk to my nose instead of to me. I have to remind myself that these thoughts are in my mind and that I'm the only one who can change them. My present GP picked up on my psychological problems immediately once I spoke up about my loneliness.

I felt the isolation of being a patient as acutely as I felt the pain from radiotherapy, and not many people speak about this feeling, but it's real, although I know not in all cases. Other patients I've spoken to have shared similar stories. My illness may not have been as critical as many other cancers can be, even though it was very aggressive, so maybe that's why some of the professionals I saw felt I didn't need outside input as much as other patients. Who knows?

As a qualified staff nurse, I feel sad that health-care professionals let this happen, but all patients experience setbacks and problems. Nothing is perfect. I have always tried to give my full loving care to my patients and their families. When I was diagnosed, for the first time, I was the one being cared for; I was the patient managing a life-altering condition. This episode of my life has given me further insight into just what health-care workers put people through. Looking back on my treatment, I've wondered, did I make my patients feel unwanted or frightened? Did I make them feel like they'd asked too much of me?

But being positive is a central part of my make-up now. It has to be able if I'm to cope with cancer and its treatment. When I was still working, the importance of positivity I had learnt from my experience as a patient helped me to better treat my patients with or without cancer. My experience also taught me how other people's attitudes affect a patient's state of mind. My colleagues offered me love, care, and support. My ward sisters, managers and colleagues are the most fantastic group of people I have ever had the pleasure to work for because of their love and support. I thank them with all my being.

But I feel an important part of my life was taken away when I retired, and sometimes I've felt angry because I had to give up after working so hard to achieve the nursing levels I achieved. I loved being a nurse. I had the pleasure of passing on what I had achieved and learnt over the years about caring for patients through teaching student nurses and other nurses. This wasn't just a job; it was a career.

My journey has gone on longer than I had hoped it would, but I have been in remission for two years now, and if I'm lucky, god willing, I will make it another three years and be free of cancer. That seems like a lifetime away, but I know it's not, sometimes it feels like a noose hanging around my neck and I'm certainly not going to give up before I get there. Until then, I will carry on with my operations until the plastic surgeon decides he is finished. I will go to my appointments as required. But I will also enjoy my family, friends, and the new life I'll make for myself outside nursing. I intend to stay in touch with my colleagues on the ward, and, if I can, I'll volunteer there sometimes or just stop in to have a cuppa with the girls.

I've been busy having a lot of fun with family and friends, and my hubby loves the fact that he never knows what I'm going to do next. "It's the spice of life," I say to him. I have never had any regrets about the past, and I'll never let this episode ruin the rest of my life. Who knows what the future will bring, none of us knows but my future will be what I make it.

ABOUT THE AUTHOR

My name is Frances Moult, and I am fifty-five years old. I live in the UK, and I have been married for thirty-five years and have four children and three grandchildren. We are a happy, close family and have the pleasure of many close friends, without whom I would probably have sunk under the pressure of having cancer, going through treatment, and experiencing the fallout afterwards.

ABOUT THE BOOK

This is the first time I have ever attempted to write a book, it was inspired by a conversation with my boss while I was working as a staff nurse in the NHS after I was diagnosed with cancer. This book chronicles my journey since my cancer diagnosis, including its ups and downs and the pain and the joy I and the people I care about have experienced.